PRAYING TO WIN

*This book is dedicated to Betty,
my friend and sister in the Lord.*

The Bible referenced is the King James Version.

Copyright © 2019 Dr. Cole Roberts. All rights reserved.
No part of this publication may be reproduced, distributed, or transmitted in any form or by any means, including photocopying, recording, or other electronic or mechanical methods, without the prior written permission of the author, except for brief excerpts in reviews and certain other noncommercial uses permitted by copyright law.

coleroberts2015@gmail.com

Produced by Sea-Hill Press Inc.
www.seahillpress.com

ISBN: 978-1-7336716-0-6

Printed in the United States of America

PRAYING TO WIN

DR. COLE ROBERTS

Dr. Cole Roberts

Dr. Roberts received his B.S. degree from Western Kentucky University in 1967 and his advanced degree from Auburn University in 1971. His life has been one of searching and discovery. He sought Jesus, found him, fought with him, ran from him, and crawled back to him. The day he discovered that Jesus loved him unconditionally changed his life forever. That discovery came unexpectedly through a prayer. He wants all people to discover the secrets of prayer so they may be blessed as he has been. He has written one other book, *What If*, published by Westbow Press in 2015.

Acknowledgments

My special thanks to Betty, a woman whose prayers led to this book;

to Sarah, who shared her stories;

to Larry, who is a very special person;

to Samuel and Olu, who have prayed for my protection in this endeavor;

to Melody, whose baptism in the Holy Spirit is an answer to my prayers;

to Barry, who is a man of wisdom and someone whom I appreciate;

to Carolyn, for insisting I go deeper in my explanations;

to Clancie, who gave me a quick lesson in the art of writing introductions;

to Linda, who was kind enough to read a rough manuscript;

to Glen, who gave me some good advice;

to Suanne, my patient wife; and

to Ron, a man who understands me.

Contents

Introduction	xi
Chapter 1 *Getting Started*	1
Chapter 2 *Praying with Purpose*	9
Chapter 3 *The Kingdom*	17
Chapter 4 *Understanding the Kingdoms*	21
Chapter 5 *Know Thy Enemy*	29
Chapter 6 *The Little Ds*	39
Chapter 7 *The Well-dressed Warrior*	45
Chapter 8 *The Model Prayer*	51
Chapter 9 *Praying for Forgiveness*	63
Chapter 10 *Thy Will Be Done*	71
Chapter 11 *Lead and Deliver*	77
Chapter 12 *Facing the Demons*	85
Chapter 13 *Thine Is*	99
Chapter 14 *Healing the Wounds*	109
Chapter 15 *Praying to Win*	127
Conclusion	133
Recommended Reading	137

Old Testament

Am	Amos
1 Chr	1 Chronicles
2 Chr	2 Chronicles
Dn	Daniel
Dt	Deuteronomy
Eccl	Ecclesiastes
Est	Esther
Ex	Exodus
Ez	Ezekiel
Ezr	Ezra
Gn	Genesis
Hb	Habakkud
Hg	Haggai
Hos	Hosea
Is	Isaiah
Jer	Jeremiah
Jb	Job
Jl	Joel
Jon	Jonah
Jo	Joshua
Jgs	Judges
1 Kgs	1 Kings
1 Kgs	2 Kings
Lam	Lamentations
Lv	Leviticus
Mal	Malachi
Mi	Michah
Na	Nahum
Neh	Nehemiah
Nm	Numbers
Ob	Obediah
Prv	Proverbs
Ps	Psalms
Ru	Ruth
1 Sm	1 Samuel
2 Sm	2 Samuel
Sg	Song of Solomon
Zec	Zechariah
Zep	Zephaniah

New Testament

Acts	Acts of the Apostles
Col	Colossians
1 Cor	1 Corinthians
2 Cor	2 Corinthians
Eph	Ephesians
Gal	Galatians
Heb	Hebrews
Jas	James
Jn	John (Gospel)
1 Jn	1 John (Epistle)
2 Jn	2 John (Epistle)
3 Jn	3 John (Epistle)
Jude	Jude
Lk	Luke
Mk	Mark
Mt	Matthew
1 Pt	1 Peter
2 Pt	2 Peter
Phlm	Philemon
Phil	Philippians
Rv	Revelation
Rom	Romans
1 Thes	1 Thessalonians
2 Thes	2 Thessalonians
1 Tm	1 Timothy
2 Tm	2 Timothy
Ti	Titus

Introduction

Have you ever wanted a reset button that would allow you to start over? Have you wished that your life had no need for resets? Wouldn't it be nice if every day in your life was a day of victory? If I could show you how to make that happen, would you invest an hour of your day to have that win?

Have you ever wanted a friend who would listen to your deepest secrets and not judge you? Wished for someone who would put their arm around you no matter how badly you had treated them?

I have a friend who is never too busy to listen. He understands when I have had a bad day. When I rejoice, he rejoices with me. When I cry, he cries with me. When I am hungry, he feeds me. When I am sick, he lifts me up. I seek his counsel, and he gives me advice. I cry out for help, and he is there for me.

Do you have a friend like that? If you don't, I want to share mine with you. His capacity is unlimited. He will be a friend to anyone who will be his friend. His arms are open to everyone who wants to share in his life. I know he wants to share in yours. He is the kind of friend who will never let you down; one who will love you no matter what. When he puts his arm around someone, all the fear, frustration, and concerns just melt away. A friend like that is the most precious gift a person can receive. I want to show you how to get to know my friend, and how you can have him as yours.

These pages share how Jesus came to be my good friend. They show how you can get to know him: by doing what many Christians have not yet learned to do. That is to pray. I attended the World School of Prayer in the 1970s. The techniques I learned there taught me to pray with power and gave me a deeper understanding, which made my prayer life more effective. I desire to teach as many people as possible those same techniques and give to them the understandings that have changed my life. Praying is something we learn to do; it is not something that comes naturally, and yet it is such a natural thing. I share what I have learned in my prayer time and suggest ways that you may be blessed in yours.

I love to pray. It is my time to be in God's presence, a time to rest in his arms. It is my opportunity to serve him and to discover his will. It is my time of worship; it allows me to express my adoration, my love for, my appreciation of, and my surrender to him. It is my time to repent from the sins I am aware of and those that I am not. It is a time in which my burdens are lifted and my hopes are encouraged. It is the most precious hour of my day.

When I am depressed and oppression is sitting heavily upon my heart, I turn to God in prayer. Praise for his goodness, mercy, love, and forgiveness lifts my spirit, renews my strength, and keeps the devil from stealing my joy.

When fear and doubt invade my thoughts, I find comfort in prayer. When I lay them at Christ's feet, he strengthens me. When I am lost and in need of direction, all I must do is look to him and listen for his voice. I praise him for his answers before they come. When those answers come, and they always do, my spirit is renewed and my strength is bolstered. Once again, the devil is defeated.

Sometimes when I am bursting with the desire to do something for the Lord, I will hear him say "No." In those moments I have learned to praise him all the more. In prayer and through the experience of a lifetime of walking with him, I have learned "No" is the best expression of his love I could receive. I thank him for keeping me from the mistakes I could so easily have made. His "No" keeps me from interfering with his will and getting in his way; it prevents me from depriving someone else of an opportunity to grow in his service.

It is hard to look objectively at oneself. In prayer, I have learned to do that. The faults that everyone else have are obvious; mine are much more difficult for me to discern. Prayer is an opportunity for discovery. In it, I learn things about myself. When I pray, I often hear myself confessing things hidden in the locked drawers of my heart, faults which have hindered my Christian walk.

As the Holy Spirit leads me in confession, I discover my own shortcomings, ones I have not seen. He has taught me to recognize my personal pride, my jealousy, my greed, and my evil desires. I ask the Lord to show me the log in my own eye before I complain about the splinter in another's eye.

Through prayer, I have learned to discern a satanic attack and to discover why Satan has permission to afflict me. I have also learned how to put a stop to it and find victory over him. In prayer, I am able to open the doors of heaven and receive the blessings available to me. I have discovered how great God's goodness is for me because I have learned to fear him and to trust him (Ps 31:19). Because I have seen him fulfill the promises he has made to me and watched the unique ways in which that was done, I know his methods are indeed higher than mine (Is 55:9), and I praise him for his wisdom and awesome power.

In the Old Testament I discover the mind of God, and in the New Testament I see his plan fulfilled; through prayer, I am a participant in that plan. I have felt how much he cares for others and his hopes for all men. I have felt his pain for the lost and his joy for those being saved. His unique touch in a moment of prayer allowed me to discover the heart and mind of Christ in a very personal and life-changing way. That moment in prayer changed my heart, and that changed everything about me.

Working for God is a blessing, but praying to God is transformative. Through prayer, he touches our spirit in extraordinary ways; he gets into the locked drawers of our heart, cleanses our wounds, and heals the long-buried hurts that keep us from being all we can be in his kingdom. In prayer, he moves the mountains that impede our progress; by prayer, we can walk through the valley of the shadow of death without fear.

I hope to inspire every reader to begin a regular regimen of prayer. I will encourage you to spend quality time with your Lord so that you will discover how to win. Christians must be taught that their battle is not with one another, but with the powers and principalities in the heavens. It is time all Christians learn to fight that war in the heavens so their battles can be won on earth. I share the secrets I have learned and give the cautions I have discovered through experience. But most of all, I try to encourage every reader to find the joy that is mine when I pray. God will bless the readers of this book.

Chapter 1
Getting Started

Because I procrastinate, for me the hardest part of writing a book is getting started. From the time God laid upon my heart the idea for this book, until I actually opened the word processor and began to type, seven years went by. I knew what the book should be about but had no idea how to write it, so I kept putting off any attempt to do so. Finally, one day in prayer, I said, "Lord, I can't write this book. Unless you show me how, I can't do it." A few days later, I suddenly saw his plan for it.

Prayer is like writing a book: at some point, we must start the process. Thinking about praying is not the same as actually praying. We wonder how we will find the time for prayer. We say to ourselves, "I don't know how to pray." Some of us think we are not worthy to come before a living God; we believe he will not hear our prayers. Some are convinced their best chance of being listened to is to invoke the help of a saint or some person entitled to approach God. Many think there is no point in prayer: God is not listening.

The best way to discover what God is doing, or will do, is to put him to the test. God looks down from heaven upon the children of men to see if any understand, to see if any seek him (Ps 14:2). Jesus said that if we ask, it will be given to us; if we seek, we shall find; and if we knock, it will be opened to us (Lk 11:9). In each of these verses, the burden of discovery is ours. Finding time is never easy. Time, like every other thing in life, must be prioritized. Decide which is more important: the ball game on TV or time with your Lord.

How much time should one set aside? How much time should someone want to spend with God? Is God only important enough for five minutes, ten or twenty minutes, or would you enjoy his company enough to spend an hour with him?

There is no hard-and-fast rule for the amount of time one should pray. The apostle Paul said that we should pray without ceasing (1 Thes 5:17). I don't think that he intended for us to stay constantly on our knees. That is impractical as well as impossible. He wanted us to continually be in contact with the Holy Spirit so that in all things we would be able to hear from God. That is, after all, what prayer does. It enables God to speak to us. It connects our spirit with his. It is not a one-way conversation.

A Relationship

Paul taught that we should pray with the help of the Holy Spirit by allowing him to take the lead in every prayer (Eph 6:18). How do we make it possible for the Holy Spirit to do that? We must develop a relationship with him. Before I go any further in this discussion, I must digress from prayer and state, what is for some, an uncomfortable truth:

There is no point in prayer if you don't have a relationship with God (Jn 9:31). The only way one can have that relationship is to recognize that Jesus died on a cross to make it possible. We must, with that understanding, invite Jesus into our heart and accept his sacrifice as our ticket to salvation and to a relationship with God. When that eternal purpose begins in us, we can—with boldness and confidence through faith in him—come before the throne of God (Eph 3:11, 12).

What is the point in praying to a God with whom you have no

relationship, or in invoking the name of his son whom you have no desire to know? If that is the case, there is only one prayer you can be sure that God will hear:

Father, I invite Jesus into my heart.
I accept his sacrifice on the cross
as my forgiveness for the sin of which I am guilty.
I ask to be a member of your kingdom,
and I invite the Holy Spirit into my heart to make that possible.

If you have prayed that prayer with sincerity, you can come boldly before the throne of God's grace to obtain mercy and help in your need (Heb 4:16). Christ himself will become your intermediary.

The Way of Prayer

With that understanding, begin your prayer process by finding a quiet place where you will not be disturbed; go to your room (Mt 6:6). I like to hear worship music playing softly in the background. For me, prayer is worship, and the right music aids in that experience. Prayer is a time of praise for who he is and a time of thanksgiving for what he is doing and for what he has done. There is no biblical recommendation for having music in the background of your prayer time. It is just my preference. The right music helps me to connect with the Holy Spirit more quickly.

In the process of learning to pray, I suggest you set aside a period of time that can be divided into four equal increments. An hour works well. At first, an hour may seem like an impossible task. You may think there is nothing you can say to God for one hour. You may be tempted to repeat yourself, as the Pharisees did (Mt 6:7). The Bible cautions that vain repetition is not necessary. God does indeed know, before we ask, what our needs are.

Jesus never said how long we must pray, but he did ask Peter, James, and John to pray with him for one hour while he was in the garden of Gethsemane (Mt 26:36, 37, 40). While he wrestled with God's will in his life, as he faced arrest and the Cross, he asked them to pray with him. Instead, they slept. When we should be praying for our victories, we sleep much of the time, as they did.

Giving Thanks

We are going to learn to pray by using this time of one hour as our guide. Start by dividing the hour into four fifteen-minute segments. Spend the first fifteen minutes giving thanks to God. Psalm 100:4 says that we should enter his gates with thanksgiving and his courts with praise. We should be singing a song of gratitude as we kneel before him. God's blessings are enough that everyone should easily find ample reasons to be thankful for fifteen minutes. In everything give thanks, for this is the will of God concerning you (1 Thes 5:18). Learn to thank him for all that happens in your day.

After you thank him for the good things, thank him for all the bad stuff as well. How can I do that? Say, "God, I didn't much care for this or that, but I know that in your will you can turn it into something good in my life because I do love you and do want to be called according to your purpose" (Rom 8:28).

Of course, that means that you do love him and do want to be called according to his purpose. If you are a new Christian and aren't familiar with the many verses of the Bible which speak of thanksgiving, remember to be thankful in all things, both the good and bad. Ask the Lord to give you a grateful heart when you pray, and he will.

On occasion, I will emphasize the importance of quoting scripture. If you are a new Christian, having a limited knowledge of scripture, I encourage you to attend a new believers class in your church, or if your church doesn't have one, to find a church that does. New believers should be taught, by old believers, in the fundamentals of Christian living, including scriptures that we all should commit to memory. If you cannot attend a new believers class, I encourage you to read the Psalms and to incorporate their thanks and praise into your prayer time.

Always spend the first fifteen minutes of your time with the Lord, thanking him in all things, especially the bad ones. From the challenges of life, we discover God's greatness and learn of his love for us. In those challenges, we encounter his power and find reasons to praise him.

Praising Him

Now that we have spent fifteen minutes in thanksgiving, let us turn our hearts to praise. Psalm 100:4 says that we should enter his gates with thanksgiving and his courts with praise. As we come through the door of his house, our hearts should be grateful, but when we enter into the courtyard of his presence, we should be praising him. There is a difference between thanksgiving and praise. It is easy to fall back into an attitude of thanksgiving when we are praising the Lord, but praise and thanksgiving are not the same.

Thanksgiving is being grateful for what the Lord has done, is doing, and will do. Praise is acknowledging who he is and his worthiness. It puts him into a place of awe and respect in our minds. It is a statement of his superiority, his majesty, and his holiness. I must admit this step was the most difficult for me to learn. When I discovered the psalmists knew how to praise God much better than I did, I prayed those psalms.

Before beginning my prayer, and sometimes during the prayer, I read a psalm of praise, such as Psalm 99, and quote it to the Lord: "The Lord reigns: let the people tremble. The Lord is great in Zion; he is high above all the people. Let us praise your great and awesome name." There are many such psalms that we can and should quote before the great and awesome God. By doing this, we place ourselves in a position of humility and remind ourselves that he is God, and we are not. When you have spent fifteen minutes praising God, you will not use the next fifteen telling him what to do. Instead, you will spend it humbly imploring him for expressions of his grace.

Paul taught that we should always pray in the Spirit (Eph 6:18). Spending the first thirty minutes in thanksgiving and praise enables us to do that. It brings us into a place of worship and communion with God, which allows the Holy Spirit to begin revealing God's will to us.

Supplication

The third portion of our prayer time should be for our own need. It is a time of supplication, a time to ask God for our daily bread and personal growth. I again caution that repetition is not necessary. I pray for my needs by thanking God for the way he will provide for me. Instead of asking him to give me a job or give me this one or that one, I have found it more useful to say, "Thank you for the job you will provide for me, the one you want me to have." In other words, thank him for the result you are looking for and praise him for the way he will accomplish his purpose. Thank him not only for what he will achieve but praise him for the way he will do it also. Don't tell him how or when!

If your child came to you and said, "I want a bicycle; give me one now," would you be in a hurry to answer that demand? On the other hand, if that child comes to you and says, "Because you are a great and awesome father, because you have my best interest at heart, and because you have said that you will withhold no good thing from me, I am choosing to thank you in advance for the bicycle you will get for me when you decide I am ready for one," how would you respond? Whether I bought the bike or not, I would have to give the kid credit for the approach. The next time I saw one on sale, it would remind me of my child's desire.

When you approach God with a desire, don't tell him what to do. Instead, thank him for meeting your needs and affirm that he owns all things and is capable of all things; thus, meeting your needs is a simple undertaking for him. Show gratitude. Put him in the position of God, and take yourself off of his throne.

When we tell God what to do, we are putting ourselves on his throne and making him our servant. Christians frequently make that mistake when praying. We say things like, "God, take this tithe and use it for your glory." God doesn't need us to tell him how to use the tithe or to take it. Wouldn't it be more effective to say, "Thank you, Lord, for taking this tithe and using it to your glory"? Do you tell God what to do, or do you thank him for what he is doing?

When the Bible says to pray in all things with thanksgiving, it means *all* things. Learn to pray with thanksgiving for your needs. Thank God for the answer instead of telling him how to answer. The Bible says we should be anxious for nothing, "but in every thing, by prayer and supplication" (pray humbly, entreat), we should make our requests known to God (Phil 4:6). Don't dwell on the need, but give praise and be grateful to the one with the answer.

Demonstrate faith by thanking him for the way he will meet your need and for his excellent timing. God's timing is always perfect. I have never known him to be early, and I have never seen him be late. Wait patiently for him. Expressing your faith in those ways pleases God. Our faith motivates him. When you pray, remember this truth: *God can be motivated by your prayer, but he cannot be manipulated by it.*

Intercession

The final fifteen minutes should be a time of intercession. Intercession is an opportunity to bring about change in the lives of others. It is a chance to have a positive influence in the lives of your children, friends, neighbors, or even total strangers. Intercession brings a blessing into someone else's life. It is also a way to participate in that blessing.

When we pray as intercessors, we are to come boldly before the throne of grace so that we may obtain mercy and find grace in the time of need (Heb 4:16). Intercession is not the time to be humble before the Lord. It is a time of going to war. It requires a warrior dressed in the full armor of God to come boldly before the commander and receive instruction. By the time you have gotten to this place in prayer, you need to be dressed in the full armor of God, under the power of the Holy Spirit, and be prepared to fight (Eph 6:11).

Intercession is the time to allow the Holy Spirit to instruct you in the needs of others. When I am in this mode, I pray for the people the Lord brings into my mind and for the things he lays upon my heart. Sometimes I am surprised by the requests I make. Often, he lays upon my heart the names of people I don't know. I pray for them whether I know them or not. I pray the thoughts that come to my mind. That is praying in faith. James 5:16 says that the effectual fervent prayer of a righteous man availeth much. When we pray in the anointing of the Holy Spirit, we are righteous in the sight of God.

When we pray for others, we are standing before the throne of grace (Heb 4:16). Understand that it is a throne of mercy, not one of judgment. Be careful not to engage in judgment, but to demonstrate grace in your prayer. You should pray for someone, not about them. Rather than say, "Change his stubborn heart," ask instead that the person's spirit might be open to change. Ask that this individual may be willing and able to see what God wants to do in their lives. Instead of saying, "Make them see things my way," implore God to help both of you see things his way. When we pray about someone, we condemn ourselves. Be careful to pray for them. I will go into this in greater detail later.

Over time, following this pattern for prayer, I noticed that I was spending less time in supplication and more in intercession. As I learned to pray, I spent less time asking God to meet my daily necessities and focused instead on my spiritual needs. The extra time was devoted to praying for others. That is as it should be. We should be more interested in the needs of others than our own. God has always taken care of me. Matthew 6:8 says that God knows what my needs are before I ask him.

As I learned to trust God, my prayers focused on the needs of others instead of my own. Rather than spending valuable time on myself, I learned to thank him for meeting my needs and to praise him for the ways he will provide. I allow him to decide what my needs are. That he already knows.

Intercession is a powerful tool. Satan fears the Christian who goes to war in this manner. This is the one Christian who does bind him and does rob his house with impunity (Mt 12:29). In this type of prayer, make requests for all the saints by binding the powers of darkness while dressed in the whole armor of God (Eph 6:11-18). If you want to be a soul winner, spend time in your prayer room in supplication and intercession for the lost in general and those you know specifically.

James 5:16 says, "The effective fervent prayer of a righteous man availeth much," which means that the sincere prayer of a caring man will accomplish much because it is effective. I know a man who led 120 people to Christ in one year. He never left his home to do that, and most of them he did not know. He prayed for each of them by name daily for one year, asking God to lead them to a saving knowledge of Christ and to lay upon their heart their need for baptism. He was praying for 650 individuals daily, and out of that number, 120 of those people responded to the Lord seeking salvation and baptism.

This man never had the joy of a personal conversation with any of them; he never led any to a prayer of salvation, and yet without his prayers, they may not have been saved. One family who responded had been attending a church for fifteen years. They had never confessed their faith in the Lord or asked for baptism. This man knows the value of intercessory prayer. Would you like to be a soul winner?

Chapter 2
Praying with Purpose

"What is that noise, Daddy?" I heard my son saying, as we walked from the boat dock to the truck. Rather than answer and scare him, all I said was, "Keep on walking!" The snake was in the bushes but not on the path, and I wanted him out of that rattler's reach. I was surprised that he didn't stop in his tracks and ask why. "Why?" was his favorite question. When I hear Christians asking why, my usual answer is, "Because it could." I intend to show how that dynamic can be changed.

When trouble comes, the first question many Christians ask is, "Why did God let this happen?" Some say, "How could God let this happen?" They are implying that he isn't doing his job. I ask them why they think God let them down. I question their responsibility in this situation. Who caused the problem? Could it have been one's own fault? Is God really to blame? Is it possible some unseen force played a role in this? I ask them whether there might be a purpose for this testing time in their life, and if so, what do they think it is?

Thank You, Father

We should see everything that happens in our lives as an opportunity to give thanks and praise to God. That can be hard to do. How can I praise God when my child dies unexpectedly? Why would I be grateful for losing my job? The words "Thank you, Lord" are not the ones that come to mind when my car breaks down, leaving me stranded on the side of the road. It is hard to praise him in the midst of the storm that is blowing the roof off of my house.

I have never lost a child, but I have lost friends and relatives. I found comfort in thanking God for the time I had with them. I praised him for bringing us together and thanked him for all the memories that would go to my grave with me. When my car broke down, I praised him for the way he would bring help to me and thanked him for the protection he would give to me. After the tornado tore holes in my roof, I gave thanks and praise for the protection my family received. When I lost my job, I knelt before him and gave thanks for the way he would provide and praise for the next job I would get. When I faced death, I gave him praise for his power to heal, gave him thanks for the doctors and nurses who would attend to me, and praised him for his outcome.

Philippians 4:6 says in everything by prayer and supplication with thanksgiving, we should let our requests be made known unto God. Perhaps when things go awry, instead of blaming God, we should see all things as an opportunity to discover his grace, love, mercy, and his awesome power to bless us. Proper praying in adversity is an opportunity to see his kingdom come into our midst.

Many Christians seem to think prayer is only about receiving. Some use it as an opportunity to blame, to judge, to criticize, and to condemn others. If Christians had a better understanding of the purpose of prayer, perhaps they would not only pray differently but more often as well. It is a sad commentary to know that the average Christian prays less than three minutes per day; the average pastor, less than five. It is no wonder that Christians are powerless and churches are stagnating and ineffective.

Americans, in particular, are a people who want instant gratification with a minimum of effort. Some Christians approach prayer in the same manner. By saying, "Thank you, Father, for this food and for blessing it to the nourishment of our bodies," we expect that to be sufficient to cover our day's needs, and even more. Prayer has a purpose beyond personal needs.

Prayer is how God's kingdom is brought to earth and, most importantly, into our lives. Effective, committed prayer brings into our lives the kingdom of God. Because we Americans do not understand the nature of a kingdom, our prayers are limited to the confession of sin and requests for a blessing.

If we want to see real power in our lives, to live with authority, to walk in the footsteps of Christ, and to do the things he did, we must learn to pray as he did. We must understand that the purpose of prayer is not to bless us, but is to usher in the kingdom of God. Being blessed is a byproduct of living in his realm. Bringing the kingdom of God to earth is a Christian's responsibility. It is the ongoing work Christ delegated to us from the Cross.

In the Beginning

It is necessary to understand that God is King, and we are not. The Bible says, "In the beginning, *God* created" (Gn 1:1). It doesn't say *we* created. It means that he established this kingdom for us. It is our inheritance, created for us before "the foundations of the world" (Mt 25:34).

In the beginning, God created the heavens and the earth and all that was in them. At some point in time, he gave permission for the heavens to be separated from the earth's surface. God then declared that the waters that covered the earth should recede; as a result, dry land appeared. Then, because the planet was void of living things, he created all life, which included plants, fish, birds of the air, animals, and all living creatures (bugs and such), including an animal in human form.

But then God took that creature with the form of a person and said, "Let us create man in our image," and God breathed into him the spirit of life. He put into him a soul. At that moment, mankind took on the nature, characteristics, and essence of God. There was now a spirit living within Adam that kept him from being only an animal. Now he was like God. God placed Adam in charge of everything he had created and gave to Adam the authority to rule in his place. (Gn ch:1-2).

In the beginning, it was good. Adam lived in a perfect environment. He was living in a garden created by God. It was never too hot or too cold. Food was plentiful, and nothing was withheld from him. He had fellowship with his creator and authority over his world. In the center of that garden were two unique trees. One was the tree of life, and the other tree represented the knowledge of good and evil. God cautioned Adam and Eve not to eat of the latter because, on that day, they would surely die (Gn 2:16, 17).

Notice that God gave them a choice. They could choose to eat from the tree of life as much as they wanted, and continue to live with God forever; or they could eat from the tree of knowledge of good and evil, and die. God said they should not eat of that tree unless they wanted to die. He gave them the right to choose.

Death in that context was both spiritual and physical. Spiritual death came the moment they tasted the fruit of sin. The physical death happened later. The point that must be understood is that *to live is to be in a relationship with God; to die is to be out of fellowship with him.* God is the source of life. By him, all things were created; and in him, all live. This is why every person, and every culture (no matter how primitive), has a concept of God. Because God gave us life and is the source of life, we cling to him and long for him, even when we have never heard of him.

In the beginning, it was good. Adam and Eve lived in harmony with all the animals. They lived in peace with each other. There was no sickness and no death. Adam and Eve fellowshipped with God; the Bible says that God walked with them in the garden in the cool of the day, and on at least one occasion, he searched for them (Gn 3:8, 9). He called out to them.

Let There Be Light

The Bible says that while the earth was still without form and was void of shape because it was covered by water, God said, "Let there be light" (Gn 1:3). He called the light day and the darkness night. A superficial reading of this verse leads one to think that it only refers to day and night. More careful reading shows that the sources of light as physical entities were not created until day four. It was then that God created the sun and moon (Gn 1:14-16).

A careful reading also shows that when God created light, darkness was already present. What is it that God created on day one? Was it an idea that he conceived on day one and didn't create the source of until day four, or does it have a different meaning?

Before anything else was made, God made righteousness; he determined that his creation would be a kingdom of right-doing. The Bible says, "The Lord is my light and my salvation, whom shall I fear?" (Ps 27; 1). Psalm 119:105 says, "Thy Word is a lamp unto my feet and a light unto my path." John 1:4 says, "In him was life, and the life was the light of men." Verse 9 says, "Jesus is the true Light which lighteth every man that cometh into the world."

Light and Darkness

John 3:19 says, "This is the true condemnation that light has come into the world, and men loved darkness rather than light because their deeds were evil." Because evil was already present when God decided to make light, one should conclude the light he declared on day one was *spiritual* light, and *natural* light came into being on day four.

Darkness was already present. This begs the question, where did the evil come from? If the light is good, and its source is God, and Jesus is the light, and evil is wrong, who then is the source of evil? With whom did the darkness originate?

The apostle Paul, when he was testifying before King Agrippa, recounted his conversion and his commission to preach to the Gentiles. He said that Jesus sent him to the Gentiles to turn them from darkness to light, from the power of Satan to God, that they might receive forgiveness from sins and an inheritance among those who are sanctified by faith in him (Acts 26:15-18).

Beauty's Corruption

According to Paul, darkness is the power of Satan, and he is the source of darkness. Satan was present before the creation of the garden and of man. The Bible describes him as an anointed cherub that was perfect in every way until iniquity was found in him. It says he was in the Garden of Eden, and because his own beauty corrupted him, he decided to place his throne above that of God (Ez 28:12-19, Is14:12-14). Pride goes before a fall.

The Bible describes cherubs as winged guardians, angels who were the closest to God's throne (Gn 3:24; Ez 10:3-22). This cherub decided to be above God. He wanted to be a god himself. Some scholars say that jealousy arose in him because God made man higher in his esteem than he made the angels (Heb 2:5-8). Some teach that Satan's envy appeared because God put Adam in charge of the garden instead of him. Either scenario would explain his desire to corrupt mankind. Each is a motive for what happened next.

On one beautiful day (my supposition), Satan, in the form of a serpent, was languishing in the garden in the proximity of the tree of knowledge. When Eve came by, he employed the trick that he continues to use this day: he caused her to question God's Word. "Did God really say you could not eat of any tree in the garden?" It was a seemingly harmless question. But it was a trap Eve fell into.

The Bible doesn't say what Satan was doing when this occurred; I suspect he was draped on the tree of knowledge, thus tempting Eve to add to God's Word. She told him they could eat of any tree in the garden but the tree of knowledge. She then said, "But of that one, God said, 'you shall not eat, nor shall you touch it, lest you surely die" (Gn 3:1-3). She attributed words to God that he did not say. God had made no mention of touching the tree.

The moment she made that statement, Satan was either slithering onto the tree or in some other way he was having physical contact with the tree. Because he was not dying, Eve began to compare what Satan was doing with what she had been cautioned against and started to doubt the Word of God. Satan then used the very same lie he is still using on people today: If you do this, you will be like God. He was really saying, "If you do this, you will be equal to God" (Gn 3:5).

Holy Authority

Adam and Eve were already like God, but they didn't know that. They had been created in his image. They were holy. They were pure in thought and purpose. There was no guile or deceit in them. They were perfect in every way because they had no knowledge of sin. Also, they had all control over the living creatures of the earth (Gn 1:26). They did not have jurisdiction over the planet itself but had power over everything on the earth's surface.

God had retained authority over what happened in the skies and under the earth's surface. He kept authority over the laws of physics and control of the wind and the rain. Adam and Eve had the right to make their own choices. They were free to live in the kingdom of light and receive all of the blessings that went with it *or* to choose darkness and its consequences.

Romans 11:29 says that the gifts and calling of God are irrevocable, which means that once God gives it to you, he is not going to take it back. He cannot; it is no longer his. He had delegated to Adam total authority over the things on the earth, including his own choices. The only way Adam could lose that authority was to give it away.

When Adam took a bite of the fruit, he gave away his birthright. He exchanged his relationship with God for one with Satan. He gave his allegiance to Satan. Until that time, Adam had authority over everything on the earth, including his own life. When he bit into the fruit, he exchanged his jurisdiction for servitude.

Adam surrendered all of his rights to Satan. He traded fellowship with God for the knowledge of sin. Adam lost his friendship with God because God cannot and will not look upon sin with favor. He will have no relationship with sinners; that is why he sent Christ into this world (1 Tm 1:15). He wanted to turn sinners back into saints. Sinners try to hide from him because of their wickedness, just as Adam and Eve hid after they had eaten of the fruit (Gn 3:8 Is 33:14).

Esau and Jacob

The story of Esau and Jacob is a perfect example of what happened in the garden. In the Bible there is a story of twin brothers Jacob and Esau, sons of Isaac. Esau was the oldest. In his culture, the eldest son was entitled to the estate and the father's blessing. That benefit was more valuable than the estate because it indicated the life the son was to have; it was his birthright. Esau sold his birthright for a bowl of soup.

When Esau came to receive his dying father's blessing, his father said that he had already given it to him (Gn 25:29-34). Jacob had disguised himself as Esau and tricked Isaac into giving him the blessing intended for his brother. Isaac said, "I have already made him your master." Esau pleaded for any help, so Isaac said that Esau's dwelling would be the fatness of the earth and by the sword, he would live and serve his brother. But it would come to pass that when he became restless, Esau would break Jacob's yoke from his neck.

This is the very same thing that happened in the garden. Esau's ancestor Adam did the same thing for a taste of forbidden fruit. These men relinquished their inheritance for a bite. Neither appreciated their loss until it was too late. The only difference being that for Adam there was no blessing, only a curse.

Redemption

God's plan provides a way for mankind to reclaim what was theirs in the beginning. That plan involves a sacrifice of blood, willingly given for the sake of all people. At the appointed time, God had his own son become that sacrifice so that mankind can legally reclaim from Satan what Adam had freely given away (Jn 3:16).

Because Adam was the first man, when he gave away his birthright, it included the heritage of all who followed. When Jesus died on the Cross to redeem our inheritance, it could only apply to one person at a time. Just as one man made for himself the choice to follow Satan, so must all other men make a decision to follow Christ.

The Fight for Birthright

Like Esau, we cannot break the yoke of Satan from our necks until we pick up the sword and start to fight back. We cannot regain the kingdom promised to us from the beginning without a fight. Satan will not turn it loose without one.

Prayer is the battleground of redemption. We reclaim the kingdom of God through prayer. We claim salvation and the right to a relationship with God through Christ on the Cross, but we regain that relationship through prayer. The subsequent chapters of this book will show how that is done.

Chapter 3
The Kingdom

When the disciples asked Jesus to teach them to pray, he showed them to pray for the kingdom to come (Mt 6:10). As I have said, Americans don't grasp the concept of a kingdom. Perhaps we should look at it more in light of our own thinking. We believe that each person has the right to choose. We make our own choices and thus declare ourselves king. We feel that our homes are our castles, and in them, we are the king. We say that we are in charge of our own destiny. That is the declaration of a king. Most of us are willing to fight to protect what is ours, which is the responsibility of a king. The head of every household makes the decisions for the family. That is the prerogative of a king.

Obedience to the King

My household lived by a set of principles. I declared that we would follow certain precepts, live according to what were acceptable principles of behavior, and I determined the rules of conduct. I enforced the laws and rewarded obedience to them. There was harmony in our home when those laws were followed.

From time to time, discord occurred, especially when my children became teenagers. They felt that they could make their own choices and decide which rules to follow. Sometimes their decisions led to trouble. At times it became necessary for me to intervene. Sometimes I waited for them to seek my advice. Unfortunately, many times when they got themselves into trouble, instead of asking for my guidance, they tried to hide their problems from me. In those instances, they endured inner turmoil. "What is going to happen if Daddy finds out?" At other times, they feared their punishment more than they regretted their actions.

In some instances, they didn't want to see my disappointment. They didn't want me to know they had let me down by failing to live up to the principles of our home. They didn't want me to discover they weren't perfect. At times, their friends were the problem. Peer pressure is a powerful force in our children's lives. Some of their friends came from homes without fathers. Those children had no father to influence them or to lay down laws to be followed. Their influence, in some instances, led my children to question the wisdom of following my rules.

My mistakes and failures caused them to question my authority. My inability to show compassion, love, understanding, and grace caused them to perceive me as an unworthy king. The subjects of such a king feel he is not deserving of respect. They see no reason to obey him. When the king's robes aren't clean, his people see no point in keeping theirs clean.

Being a king is no easy task. Running a kingdom is difficult. Because each subject doesn't sit with the king and discover him on a personal level, they can't understand his reasoning; they can only observe him and render judgment of him. When our children don't come to us, we can't explain to them our concern. When they only see rules, they don't understand the purpose for them. They don't realize that our love is the reason for them. They fail to comprehend that these principles are there to protect them and to keep them in good stead in our family. They don't understand that broken statutes lead to strained relationships.

They aren't aware that a good father only wants the best of everything for his children. In these instances, the father must stand his ground and hope that with maturity his children will gain the wisdom to understand why he had to insist on certain principles. Sometimes the only thing a father can do is release his children to their own will and hope that, before it is too late, they will come to their senses and return home (Lk 15:11-32).

Kingdom Authority

Perhaps looking at our life and our home will make it easier to understand the concept of the kingdom to which Jesus referred. As he walked with his disciples, he taught them about the one that was coming. As most children do, they misunderstood much of what he was saying. They were looking forward to an immediate kingdom, while Jesus was talking of one that was coming in two phases.

The first came after Jesus died on the Cross and was resurrected. It happened when the Holy Spirit invaded the hearts of those Christians in the upper room (Acts 2:1-4). Our baptism in the Holy Spirit enables us to live in the kingdom of God. Jesus was also talking about the final one that would come when he returns again. That will happen when Jesus returns to earth to rule in righteousness with all authority, and at that time all men will bow before him and confess that he is Lord (Rom 14:11).

Our immediate concern should be for the first kingdom to come, the one we are to usher into our lives each time we pray, the one Jesus told us to pray for. The Bible refers to the kingdom of heaven, the kingdom of God, and Christ refers to his kingdom. There is no significant difference between them. The kingdom of heaven is located in the heavenly realm where God reigns; it is the kingdom that he reigns over now.

The kingdom of God is the one that is to be established in each of us when Jesus becomes our Lord and when we are baptized in the Holy Spirit; it is the power of God living in us now. Romans 14:17 says that kingdom is not meat and drink, but it is righteousness, peace, and joy in the Holy Spirit. The kingdom of God is not what we take in but what we have in us. Meat and drink do not sustain or satisfy us, but it is righteous living that leads to the peace with God that gives our hearts joy. It is doing what is right that allows us to live in harmony with our God, that enables us to live in God's kingdom now.

The kingdom of God is one of power through the Holy Spirit. It is the power to witness and do the works of Jesus (Acts 1:8). Christ's kingdom is the kingdom he will establish when he returns to earth as King. It is the one he will establish at his second coming, sometimes referred to as the millennial kingdom.

When Adam and Eve lived in the garden, they were living in the kingdom of heaven on earth. The garden was a reflection of God's heavenly kingdom. It was a place of beauty; harmony existed between all of God's creation and all of his living things. It was a place of relationships.

Adam had authority over the animals, and as the story of the serpent shows, man and animal communicated with each other; but most importantly, it shows that Adam and Eve spoke to God daily. He walked and talked with them every day. They discovered his will, got to know his desire for the garden, and had fellowship with him. They never experienced sickness, had all that they needed to eat, and required no shelter from the elements. Because they were in his kingdom, they knew only peace and joy. Nothing was lacking in their life, and it was everlasting.

The garden is an example of the kingdom of heaven that believers will inherit. Heaven is a place of eternal beauty in the presence of God. It is also a place of harmony and abundance, having God as King and Jesus as Lord. The kingdom of God Jesus referred to is a representation of the kingdom of heaven. It is his kingdom living in us now. When Adam ate of the forbidden fruit, he gave his authority, which was granted to him by God, to Satan. When Christ died on the Cross, he reclaimed for man the right to take back from Satan the kingdom through a relationship with himself. He gave people the power to re-establish God's kingdom in their own lives.

Kingdom Come

The fullness of God's kingdom will not happen until Christ returns to earth physically as the King of kings (Rv 17:14, 19:16). When he returns to reign with all power and authority, God's kingdom, as intended in the garden, will be restored. Until then we can enjoy God's kingdom in our own lives through a relationship with Jesus Christ. It is not a kingdom of weakness, of sickness, of doing without. It is a kingdom of power, of authority, of fullness. It is a kingdom of war and conflict, but it is also one of peace and joy. It is a kingdom in which warriors reign and rule. Teaching the reader how to do that is the purpose of this book.

Chapter 4
Understanding the Kingdoms

As previously stated, the purpose of prayer is to bring in the Kingdom of God. Because many Christians don't understand what God's Kingdom is, they don't know what that statement means. When Jesus was on trial for his life, Pilate asked, "Are you the king of the Jews?" (Jn 18:33) Jesus said that his kingdom was not of this world (Jn 18:36). When Pilate asked him if he were a king, meaning any king, Jesus answered yes. He said that he was a king. Jesus came into the world for this cause that he should bear witness to the truth, and that everyone who receives the truth would hear his voice (Jn 18:37).

Repentance

What is the truth men receive? The first truth is that the kingdom of God is at hand (Mk 1:15). The prelude to that truth is how Jesus began his ministry: by preaching, "Repent for the kingdom of heaven is at hand" (Mt 4:17). Repentance is required before mankind can enter into God's kingdom. We must turn our backs on sin before we can enter into the realm that Jesus brought to earth and the heavenly one to come.

Repentance means to turn away from, to change one's mind. The truth that Jesus taught has no room for sin. The heart Jesus lives within cannot hold onto sin and expect to be filled with righteousness. We enter the kingdom with repentance and live in it by grace. Paul taught that the kingdom of God is righteousness, peace, and joy in the Holy Spirit (Rom 14:17).

Righteousness is doing what is right in God's sight. We do that by and through the Holy Spirit living in us. When our hearts want what he deems as proper, inner peace is our reward. Joy is the result of that. The angry man has no peace. The lustful man has no joy. The jealous person is never content. Sinners know they are unrighteous. Because of that, they live in fear of judgment instead of having the inner tranquility that comes from forgiveness (Is 2:10, 29:15; Rv 6:16).

A King's Likeness

A kingdom is a reflection of its king. Nations, towns, businesses, and homes are all a reflection of the person ruling them. Countries ruled by tyrants become nations of slaves. Cities ruled by dishonest leaders are citadels of greed and corruption; in them, power is sold by politicians and bought by the wealthy. Which cities in America do you think are examples of crime, corruption, and immorality? What patterns do their leaders set? Do you think those leaders are more interested in their purse than their purpose?

The Spirit that Leads

Think of the Presidents who have been in office during your lifetime. What was our country like during their time in office? Putting politics aside, can you think of one who had a problem with the truth? Why do you think people distrust government? Have you felt that any of the Presidents in your lifetime were incompetent? Did that cause you to believe the government was the problem instead of the solution? Have any inspired you to hope for the future? What do you think caused Americans to become so divided? Could it be the examples the men in the White House have set? The character of a leader affects the nature of a nation, state, town, company, family, etc. That character is a reflection of the spirit motivating them.

Every nation, state, and municipality is ruled by a demonic spirit. Remember, Satan is the ruler of this world (Jn 12:31, 14:30, 16:11). Some states are ruled by a spirit of jealousy. Their people are never happy for another's success. They feel obligated to outdo one another. More than one western state is ruled by a spirit of apathy. For someone with a Type-A personality, like mine, that isn't entirely a bad thing. For the population as a whole, it is. In those states, mediocrity is the highest goal sought by many.

People from a particular part of California can be recognized by their greed. There is a region of a northern state that is ruled by a spirit of aggression. When these people come to Florida in the winter, that spirit manifests itself. They impatiently blow their horns, get into arguments, and run red lights. Their anxiety reminds me of a rubber band twisted to its breaking point.

I once lived in a state ruled by a false sense of pride. It caused people there to look down on others. It encouraged them to think they were better than those less fortunate. Instead of holding others in higher esteem than themselves, they saw them as lesser persons and treated them with scorn and contempt. One town in Oregon inspired a book about a place where a spirit of witchcraft was prevalent. Think about the nature of your city or state. That is the kind of demon motivating its citizens.

Head of the Family

Just as every nation and every part of a country is affected by one of Satan's demons, every family is denoted by its governing spirit. For some families that may be pride, greed, or envy; for others, it could be adultery, fornication, or pornography; and some may be controlled by one of alcoholism or drug addiction. Are any of these traits present in your family? The women in my mother's family wore pride and greed as badges of honor, and I am sorry to say, in some cases, those traits have passed to their children.

Homes led by unchristian parents raise children with no respect or consideration for God. Those children display ungodly character as adults. Evil prevails in their lives. Christian families aren't immune from struggles, but they have a source of redemption. Satan's kingdom is characterized by the demons in charge. It is one of despair and hopelessness. God's kingdom is one of hope and redemption.

Free Indeed

Jesus came to establish a kingdom freed from these demons and their influence. His is a kingdom of righteousness, characterized by peace and joy within us. Jesus compared the kingdom to seeds. Some are sown on rocky soil, some on shallow ground, and some in good soil. In the right soil, they spring up, and a crop is produced (Mt 13:3-9). The seeds of the kingdom will sprout in some people and not in others. In some people, they will take root but will quickly be overtaken by weeds (demons) and die from a lack of nutrient. Which kind of person are you?

Jesus taught that his kingdom is like a treasure that has been hidden. When it is found, that person sells everything that he has to buy the field where it is located (Mt 13:44). Jesus compared it to a pearl of great price. When discovered, a man would sell all that he had to possess it (Mt 13:45, 46). How much would you pay to have an inner peace that surpasses all understanding (Phil 4:7)?

Jesus also taught that the seeds of his kingdom would have to coexist with the weeds sown by the wicked one until the harvest. He said the devil sowed the tares who are his sons, that the harvest is at the end of this age, and the reapers are the angels sent by God (Mt 13:37-39). In other words, the kingdom of God will coexist with the realm of Satan until the end, and then will come judgment.

The entire story of the Bible is a message of redemption. It is the story of the fall of mankind and of God's effort to redeem us from that fall. Through one man, sin entered the world, and death through sin entered into all people (Rom 5:12). Through Jesus and his righteous acts, the free gift of grace came to all people (Rom 5:18).

Through Grace

Those who accept God's grace, which is the gift of eternal life given to us by Christ on the Cross, have the right to live in the kingdom of God here on earth and, at the appointed time, in heaven itself. God gave the law to Moses so that the children of Israel could live in his kingdom here on earth. They were required to obey the Ten

Commandments, which would lead them to holiness and enable them to live in righteousness. As Adam did, they failed to comprehend the words of life that God gave to them. They were unable to achieve righteousness, which they sought through works because they did not seek it by faith (Rom 9:30-32).

Walking with the Holy Spirit

When Jesus died on the Cross, he gave to mankind the opportunity to obtain righteousness and, as a result, the right to live in his kingdom. We are saved by grace through faith, not of works lest any should boast. It is the free gift of God (Eph 2:8). What we cannot accomplish through the law, we can do through the Holy Spirit when we walk with him (Rom 8: 3-4).

When Christ ascended to heaven, he sent to us the Holy Spirit whom he called another Comforter or Helper (Jn 14:7-11) so that, through him, the laws of Moses would be written into our hearts, and through faith, we would fulfill them. In doing that, we live in righteousness; by that, we live in the kingdom of God. Those who are led by the spirit are the children of God (Rom 8:14).

Wielding the Sword

The kingdom of heaven belongs to the sons of God, but they must take it by force (Mt 11:12). The sons of Satan have a grip on this world and all who are in it. God's people must wrestle his kingdom from their grasp. This is done through the power of prayer. In prayer, we bind the devil and loot his house (Mk 3:27).

The kingdom of God is power. It is the power to live a righteous life under the influence of the Holy Spirit. He gives us the authority to cast out demons and the ability to speak in new tongues, to withstand Satan and his henchmen, to resist deadly teaching and temptation, and to lay hands on the sick and see them recover (Mk 16:17-18). Of course, these things only occur in those who believe, and only through the name of Jesus.

When the believing Christian wields the name of Jesus, strongholds will fall. Those Christians who believe in him will do the works he did, and even greater works (Jn 14:12). What did Jesus do? He restored sight to the blind, the spiritually blind and the physically blind.

He made the cripple to walk. Jesus raised the dead, the physically and the spiritually dead. He cleansed the lepers. And he preached the gospel to the poor, the financially poor and the poor in spirit (Lk 7:22).

Jesus promised to do whatever we asked in his name so that the Father might be glorified by the Son (Jn 14:13). Two things can keep this from happening: One is the lack of belief, and the other is our failure to ask.

Sons and Daughters

When Jesus died on the Cross for us and was resurrected from the dead, he ascended to heaven so that he could send us the Holy Spirit. Those who receive Christ as savior, even those who just believe in his name, have the power to become the sons and daughters of God (Jn 1:12, 13). Notice these verses say "power to become." The ones who do become are those who are led by the Spirit. They are the children of God (Rom 8:14). Those who learn to wield the sword of the Spirit bring the kingdom of heaven to earth and possess the power of God.

I should point out that five steps are involved in becoming a mature son or daughter of God:

1. The understanding that there is a God is the first step. You must believe in the God of the Bible not just in a higher power.

2. When you comprehend the plan of salvation, you must invite Christ to be your personal savior and Lord.

3. After Christ enters one's heart, they must learn to hear his voice. Jesus said, "My sheep hear my voice, and I know them, and they follow me" (Jn 10:27). Notice that Jesus did not say my lambs. Sheep is the term applied to mature animals. Understand that those who hear are obligated to follow.

4. We learn to trust God when we follow him. When we listen, he instructs us. As we follow the Lord and see his outcome, we discover that his promises are fulfilled, and we learn to trust him. Abraham spent twenty-five years following God, waiting on his promised son and seeing God's power to protect him in all circumstances. In that, he learned to trust God (Gn 12: 1-3, 10-20).

5. Those who learn to trust God know to obey him. When God told Abraham to offer his promised son on an altar, Abraham was obedient. The Bible says that he had the faith to believe God would resurrect Isaac in order to fulfill his promise (Heb 11:17-19).

The Sword of the Spirit

The mature Christian who has learned to hear, trust, and obey God can wield the sword of the Spirit—which is the Word of God—with accuracy, with authority, and effectively. Their feet are shod in the gospel of peace; they wear the helmet of salvation and the breastplate of righteousness; they carry the shield of faith because their loin is covered by the girdle of truth.

When mature Christians speak, the demons recognize their authority. Instead of hearing the demons say, "Jesus I know, but who are you?" (as one did when the sons of Sceva tried to exorcise it); those demons will obey your command, in the name of Jesus (Acts 19:13-15).

If you want to be the warrior Christ envisioned, it is imperative that you understand the principles of the kingdom and understand who the enemy is. It is necessary to be dressed in the whole armor of God. The next chapters of this book will show how to take the fight to the enemy.

Chapter 5
Know Thy Enemy

I have heard it said that Americans like to fight. I don't think that is true, but I do believe we want to win when we fight. Conflicts end in one of three ways: win, lose, or draw. For most people, winning is the goal. No one sets out to fail. Unfortunately, some people think a draw is acceptable.

Our most popular sports are fought with the goal of winning. A draw is not acceptable. When these games end in a tie, overtime is declared, and the game continues until a victory is concluded. For the first two hundred years of this nation, all our wars were fought with the goal of winning.

A Negotiated Loss

Beginning with the Korean War, that goal changed to keeping the status quo. Winning was no longer the objective. Our leaders were content to declare a stalemate as a win. We learned nothing from that war. We are still paying for that mistake sixty-five years later. We have spent billions of dollars trying to keep the truce we negotiated. A victory would have been much less expensive. We would not be faced with the possibility of a nuclear war with the North Koreans today if we had possessed the resolve to win.

What we declared as a stalemate in Vietnam was, in reality, a loss. It has been far less expensive than the deadlock we settled for in Korea. Our most significant sacrifice was the sixty thousand American lives and the countless Vietnamese lives lost for a war we never intended to win.

When President George H. W. Bush ran Saddam Hussein from Kuwait, he stopped at the border of Iraq. The resolve to liberate Kuwait was actually his desire to maintain the status quo. When George W. Bush invaded Afghanistan, most Americans cheered him on and thought it was a war we would win. When he invaded Iraq, some people said he was cleaning up his father's mess. When that invasion appeared to be a victory, Barack Obama gave it away. Some students of prophecy believe his decisions allowed the beginning of the march to Armageddon.

All In for the Win

Wars are won, lost, or fought to surrender as the result of three things. The outcome depends upon resources, resolve, and knowledge of the enemy. Christians have an abundance of resources. All things are possible through Christ who strengthens us (Phil 4:13). Our God owns the cattle on a thousand hills (Ps 50:10). He will give us all the resources we need to win the fight; all we must do is ask (Jn 16:23).

Settling for the Status Quo

It is said that the South lost the Civil War because of a lack of material resources. That was most certainly a contributing factor, but it was not the only cause. If Robert E. Lee, the general who was thought by many as the best of either army, had invaded the North in the early days of the war and destroyed their cities and their manufacturing capacity, the South could have won. I think Lee had mixed emotions. He had been a Colonel in the Union army and had been willing to die for the

United States; he was also a loyal son of the South. I suspect Lee hoped for a solution that would allow the South to be the South, and one that would keep the Union intact. It appears he failed to understand the resolve of the North to win.

It seems that the South thought a show of force would cause the North to negotiate a truce so that the status quo could continue. They fought a defensive war they hoped would lead the enemy to settle. The result was the bloodiest war in American history. Many Christians do that daily. Instead of fighting an offensive war, they remain on the defensive and wonder why they have no victories.

Underestimating the Enemy

In the Revolutionary War, Lord Cornwallis thought his troops were invincible. They had defeated the leading armies of Europe, and the British flag was flying around the entire world. His arrogance and hubris caused him to believe that the Americans were undisciplined farmers and rabble who were not worthy to take the field against his regulars. He thought his seasoned troops were worthy of better opponents. His lack of appreciation for the tactical skills of George Washington became his undoing. He suffered defeat and sailed back to England in humiliation. He didn't understand the enemy. He didn't appreciate our ancestor's resolve to win. Good can only overcome evil by virtue of our resolve.

Winning the Victory

It seems to me that Christians are making these same mistakes. We do not have the resolve to win.

I recently read a poll asking people if they believed in God. Less than 20 percent of them had faith in the God of the Bible. Some said they trusted in a higher power, but not in the God of the Bible. Some of those who trusted in the God of the Bible did not believe in his power. I found it interesting that no questions were asked about people's belief in evil. We do not understand our enemy.

I have read commentaries saying the acts of Jesus regarding demons were nothing more than him catering to a first-century superstition. I question why God would cater to superstition. As we saw in the earlier chapter of this book, in our discussion of Genesis chapters one and two, evil was already present when God decided to create light. The fact that Christians fail to believe in the absoluteness of God explains why many do not comprehend the reality of evil.

Maladies of Evil

In this day and time, the acts of Satan and his henchmen are considered diseases, maladies that need treating by medicine and therapy. Acts of evil are nothing more than society's failure to recognize the needs of those committing the act. We make excuses such as, "They were born that way." We say things such as, "They can't help themselves," or "That is the way the whole family acts; they all have problems with addictions."

People make all sorts of excuses without asking why. Why does this keep happening? Why did it start in the first place? Why does my child act this way? Why is my family falling apart? Schizophrenics are drugged into a stupor or in extreme cases locked away in a place of confinement for treatments that don't work. Sex addicts undergo counseling that help them understand their desire but do nothing to eliminate the craving.

Alcoholics and drug addicts suffer rehab repeatedly without finding a way out of their addiction. Serial killers have no remorse, just a desire to continue killing. No one looks at the spiritual reason for the problems these victims of Satan are having. Why would they? When people don't believe in God, why would they believe in Satan?

What does it take to get people to believe in God? I know what it took for me to have faith. It took an act of God and the giving of a gift that only he could give me. I can say that a similar experience caused me to realize Satan is real and powerful. What are your beliefs? How committed are you to them?

Overcomers

Do you consider God as a higher power, or do you believe in the God of the Bible? Do you think that Jesus lived and then died on a cross? Do you trust that he was raised from the dead and ascended to the right hand of God in heaven (Jn 20:17)? If you can't believe these truths, there is no reason to read this book apart from curiosity. On the other hand, if you believe in a living God and a resurrected son, you must read this book carefully. You need to know the enemy and how to overcome him.

As we saw in an earlier chapter, Satan was a cherub. He was one of God's special angels, one of those who protected the very throne of God. Because sin was found in him, he was cast from heaven and caused many other angels to be cast out as well.

Since that time he has acquired many names. He is called the god of this world in 2 Corinthians 4:4. The Bible has other names for him as well. He is called evil spirit (1 Sm 16:14); the devil (Mt 4:1); the enemy (Mt 13:39); the father of lies (Jn 8:44); adversary (1 Pt 5:8); Abadddon and the angel of the bottomless pit (Rv 9:11); and accuser of the brethren (Rv 12:10). Each of these titles is a reference to his character.

If we are going to learn how to fight, we must first understand who we are fighting. Paul said that we do not wrestle against flesh and blood but against powers, principalities, rulers of darkness in this age, and against spiritual hosts of wickedness in heavenly places (Eph 6:12). We are fighting against Satan and his demons, not against other people. Christians must understand the neighbor is not the enemy. Satan is the one we fight. He is behind everything wicked.

Understanding that Satan is the source of all evil things is a daunting task for some. In this day and age, we are too sophisticated to believe such superstition. If you are one of those, continue along the path you are on and discover how well that works for you. When those who do believe grasp the lessons in the next chapters of this book, they will be equipped to win.

Tactics of the Foe

Satan has not changed his tactics since the Garden of Eden. Why should he? They are still working. He has added some additional lies, but the tactics are the same. He works through doubt, deception, and lies. He finds a weakness and plants the seeds of temptation. Because Adam gave his soul to Satan, Satan knows that all men who are the offspring of Adam have his faults. In the beginning Adam was like God; in the end, his character was Satan's.

Jesus in the Wilderness

We can study Satan's methods best by looking at Jesus in the wilderness. The story begins in Matthew chapter three. Jesus came to Galilee to be baptized by John in the Jordan River (Mt 3:13). John was reluctant because he felt that Jesus should be baptizing him. To understand this, we need to see the purpose of John's baptism. It was a baptism of repentance for sin (Mt 3:11). In no way did it forgive sin. It was a statement of one's turning away from the sin in their life.

When Jesus asked for baptism, John understood that Jesus was the more righteous of the two. John was his cousin and knew of the circumstance of his birth. He knew him well enough to recognize his character, and he knew in his heart that Jesus was destined for greater things.

John delivered a message of repentance and told of the one to come, the one who would save the world. He went crying out, "Prepare ye the way of the Lord; make his paths straight" (Mt 3:3). We must read between the lines of scripture to understand what John didn't know. He didn't know who that person was. He may have suspected it was Jesus, but he was waiting for a sign that would indicate who the Messiah was.

Apparently, God had told him that sign would be the Holy Spirit descending upon someone whom he baptized. He would see a dove light upon them, and that would be the sign (Mt 3:16). I don't believe he heard the voice that spoke to Jesus, but he may have. The crowd present did not (Mt 3:17). If John had heard the voice, it is likely he would have announced to the crowd that the Messiah had come. I am also convinced that John did not know with certainty that Jesus was the one. After John was imprisoned, he sent his disciples to Jesus to ask if he was the Messiah (Mt 11:2).

Rather than answer them directly, Jesus said to go and tell John what you see and hear. He was saying, let my acts answer for me. Jesus said to tell John that the blind see, the lame walk, the deaf hear, the dead are raised, and the gospel is preached to the poor. Blessed is he who is not offended because of me (Mt 11:1-6). He was saying, if you don't believe me, believe the works I do. We must believe in Satan in the same way. Believe in the works he does.

When Jesus arose from the water, and the dove landed upon him, he heard a voice saying, "This is my beloved son in whom I am well pleased" (Mt 3:17). There is no way of knowing what Jesus knew before this point in time. He must have known about the circumstance of his birth. He may have heard the whispers of the people in his neighborhood as they murmured about his mother being pregnant before marriage. Surely, Mary and Joseph told him of his unique conception.

He had a relationship with the Holy Spirit before his baptism. John was filled with the Holy Spirit from birth (Lk 1:15). Why would God choose Jesus to be the Messiah and do any less for him? The scripture says that he grew and became strong in spirit, that he was filled with wisdom, and that the grace of God was upon him (Lk 2:40).

The reference could mean that he grew strong in the Holy Spirit or in his inner spirit. I don't know which. The Bible does say that Jesus went with his parents to Jerusalem at the age of twelve, and there he astounded the scholars of the day with his understanding and his answers to their questions about the Mosaic Law (Lk 2:46, 47). After that experience, the Bible says that Jesus increased in wisdom and stature, and found favor with God and men (Lk 2:52).

From these statements and considering that the Holy Spirit was the source of his conception, I have concluded that the experience at baptism was not his receiving the Holy Spirit but was his anointing by the Holy Spirit for service. This understanding is vital as we go into the wilderness with him.

After his baptism, the Bible says that Jesus was led straight into the wilderness. While there he fasted for forty days (Mt 4:2). Apart from a scarcity of food sources, what other reason might he have had for fasting? Why did the Holy Spirit lead him there in the first place? Verse one says that it was to be tempted by the devil. Before he could be tempted by Satan, something else had to occur. Before his baptism, Jesus had no ministry. He was a carpenter. He had stories and a sense of purpose but no real understanding of either.

When the Holy Spirit settled upon him, Jesus heard the voice saying that he was the son of God. He spent those forty days fasting and praying. The Holy Spirit was explaining to him his anointing and his purpose. Jesus proclaimed that purpose when he came out of the wilderness. He declared that the kingdom of God was at hand (Mk 1:15). He went to the synagogue in Nazareth and opened the book of Isaiah and read the following (Lk 4:18):

> *The Spirit of the Lord is upon me, because he has anointed me to preach the gospel to the poor: he hath sent me to heal the brokenhearted, to*

preach deliverance to the captives, and recovering of sight to the blind, to set at liberty them that are bruised, to preach the acceptable year of the Lord.

That was the commission Jesus was given in the wilderness. During those forty days, he was learning his mission, discovering who he really was, and being told what was required of him. When the Bible says the angels ministered unto him, they weren't giving food to him but did offer him an explanation of his ministry and his mission (Mk 1:13).

The Temptations

Why was he allowed to be tempted at the end of those forty days? The answer is simple: When we are given an anointing, which is God's authority for a job, we are tested to see if we will follow God's plan. How we do a task may possibly be more important to God than the actual job itself. If Jesus had succumbed to Satan's temptations, he would not have been the Messiah, and God would have needed to rewrite scripture.

The first temptation was a simple one. After forty days, Jesus was hungry. His mind is reeling from what he has been told. How would you respond if the Holy Spirit had just said that you were the son of God and your mission was to set the captives free, heal the sick, and to preach the acceptable year of the Lord?

How would you act if you had just been given the power to raise the dead, to command the wind and the rain, to calm the sea, and to turn water into wine, and then told to do nothing of your own will but to do only what you see the Father do and to say just what you hear the Father say (Jn 5:19, 30)?

Satan tempts everyone who becomes a son or daughter of God. Just as he did with Jesus, Satan says, if you are indeed a son or a daughter, prove it. Test the gifts God has given you. He first sows doubt about your relationship, and then he tempts you to disobedience. When Satan said, "If you are the Son of God, turn this rock into bread," Jesus wielded the sword of the spirit, which is the Word of God. He said, "It is written, man shall not live by bread alone, but by every Word that proceedeth out of the mouth of God" (Mt 4:4).

The Father of Lies

Many Christians fail to fulfill God's promises to them because they don't realize that he is capable of providing for them. *I have a family to care for. My kid is going to college; I need to work at my job as much as possible. I have a second mortgage that I must pay, not to mention the first mortgage. God can't possibly want me.* When Satan can't convince us to doubt that we are sons and daughters of God, he frequently finds it easy to convince us that God doesn't provide for his children.

When the devil lost that battle, he moved on to the next attempt. Again he got into Jesus' mind in a vision. The Bible says that Satan took him to the Holy City and set him upon a pinnacle of the temple. He may have transported Jesus to Jerusalem, but I believe that he caused him to see this temptation in his mind.

Just as he gets into our minds, he invaded the thoughts of Jesus. Once more, Satan tries to cast doubt on the genealogy of Jesus. "If you are the Son of God, cast thyself down: for it is written He shall give his angels charge concerning thee: and in their hands, they shall bear thee up lest at any time thou dash thy foot against a stone" (Mt 4:5, 6).

This time he quoted scripture to test Christ. Because Jesus had wielded the sword of the Spirit, Satan thought he could be entrapped in the same way, so he misquoted Psalm 91:11, 12, ever so slightly. In that way, he has misled many. It is one thing to quote scripture, and it is another to understand God's will in that scripture. Instead of pointing out Satan's misquote, Jesus once again wielded the sword of the Spirit. "It is written again, thou shall not tempt the Lord thy God" (Mt 4:7). Jesus knew that misusing God's power and gifts were in effect tempting him.

When we use God's gifts, test his power, no matter the reason, we had better be using them at his direction, lest we fall prey to Satan and tempt God. In the early days of the Charismatic movement in this country, I witnessed many young Christians fall into this trap. It is like a person with a new car. What good is it if it stays in the garage? How can you know how fast it goes without trying it out?

When Satan can't cast doubt on our parentage, he will tempt us to test our gifts and thus tempt God. Demonstrate that you are an empowered child of God and wait upon him. There are many ways to tempt God. Like the ones in this example, they all stem from misunderstanding scripture, not knowing his will, and acting without his direction.

In the next vision, the devil takes Jesus upon an exceedingly high mountain and shows him all the kingdoms of the world and the glory of them. This time he doesn't try to cast doubt that Jesus is the Son of God. After failing in the first two attempts, he gets to the heart of the matter. How about taking a shortcut? Satan knew why Jesus was there. He understood that Jesus could wrestle from him all that he had seduced Adam into surrendering. Satan is the god of this world. He has authority over mankind (2 Cor 4:4).

This time Satan says, I will give you all of this if you will just fall down and worship me (Mt 4:9). This is a trap that is easy to fall into. Servants in God's churches are very vulnerable to this trap. Some ministers are tempted to manipulate their people rather than wait upon God to motivate them. They build a sermon around a verse taken out of context and use it to convince their parishioners that what they are hearing is God's Word. Some use the "God told me" or the "I am the prophet" ploy. Taking a shortcut is an easy trap for anyone to fall into. How many businessmen take a shortcut that cheats their customer? How easy it is to keep the extra change the clerk returns by mistake.

If Satan could get Jesus to take a shortcut here, he wins. Jesus knew that his purpose was to reclaim the kingdom of God from Satan, and so did Satan. If he just gives Jesus these things, Christ gets what God wanted him to have and saves a lot of time and trouble in the process. If Jesus had fallen into this trap, Satan would have retained authority over mankind, but now he would have been God. Again Jesus wielded the sword of the Spirit. "Get thee hence, Satan: for it is written: Thou shall worship the Lord thy God, and he only will thou serve" (Mt 4:10). Christ understood that the one we worship is the one we serve.

Satan ensnares us through temptation, by casting doubt and with deception. When we pray while wearing the whole armor of God, he cannot trap us. When we put on that armor, we are ready for the fight. It is essential to understand the location of the battle. The contest is in the heavens (Eph 6:12). We must learn how to fight in that location if we are going to win in this one.

Chapter 6
The Little Ds

Satan is not omniscient (all-knowing), omnipresent (all-present), nor omnipotent (all-powerful), although sometimes it seems he is all of those things. He always seems to know my weakness. He knows that I can't resist pie. If I know there is a pie in the house, I can't stop thinking about it until I indulge in a slice, or eat the whole thing. It may not be Satan who actually tempts me to eat pie, I don't know. I jokingly tell my wife, the devil made me do it. I do know that Satan wants me to be unhealthy. He brought disease into this world and with it death.

The Nature of Man

Satan's goal is to destroy the kingdom God built. Instead of one ruled by grace, he desires a world ruled by his iron hand. Satan doesn't know what a person will do. Because people have inherited his character, he makes assumptions. As the father of lies, he assumes all men are liars. Being evil in every way, he knows that the nature of man is evil. Because he is a thief, he expects men to steal. Because he is a murderer, he knows what men are capable of (Jn 8:44). Satan blasphemes God, so he expects us to do the same. Because he refused to worship the one God, he knows that we are easily tempted to have other gods. He wants to be God, so he tempts us to become our own god.

He didn't honor his creator, thus he expects us to dishonor our parents as well as our God. He wouldn't worship his God and maker, so he tempts us to withhold our worship as well. His disregard for God caused him to disparage the name of God; therefore, he understands how quickly we will take God's name in vain. He covets God's throne, thus he knows how tempting it is for us to want our neighbor's possessions and be jealous of their accomplishments.

Notice that each of the characteristics listed are violations of the Ten Commandments (Ex 20:1-17). God gave these commandments to Moses and the Children of Israel so that they might have a relationship with him and with each other. He gave these commands so that they might have a full and blessed life. These Commandments are guidelines for healthy living, good relationships, and protection from sin. Satan tempts people to disobey so their relationships with each other and with God will die; to do that he needs help. Those helpers are what I call the little Ds.

Rulers of Darkness

Satan uses these demonic forces to help rule his kingdom, this world in which mankind lives. Paul refers to them as principalities, powers, rulers of the darkness of this age, and spiritual hosts of wickedness in heavenly places (Eph 6:12).

We catch a glimpse of this organization in the book of Daniel chapter ten. Daniel had been given the prophecy of seventy weeks by the archangel Gabriel, and he was praying to fully understand its meaning and the time frame of this vision. He had deprived himself of fun food, meat, and wine for three weeks while he prayed. His heart was heavy. It was as though he was in mourning because of this prophecy. He understood the vision but not the meaning (Dn 10:2). This prophecy that the archangel Gabriel had given him, left him confused and disturbed (Dn

9:21). Since that time Daniel had been praying earnestly for an answer.

Finally, a very impressive being appeared to him in a vision; this being was Christ in his pre-incarnate glory (Dn 10:4-9). The prophecy concerned him, who better to explain it? He reassures Daniel that his prayer had been heard from the first day and tells him that the answer was delayed because he had been in a fight with the prince of the kingdom of Persia for twenty-one days (Dn 10:12-13). Christ himself was being constrained by the prince of Persia. This prince of Persia opposed the message and the messenger because this message foretold the coming of Christ and the end of times.

The resistance was so strong that additional help had to be secured before Daniel could receive his answer. One of God's chief princes, Michael, had to join in the fight (Dn 10:13). These verses show that Satan has an organization just as God does. Our nation is organized into states with counties and cities, each having a governmental structure; the same can be said for the heavens.

Each nation has a ruling prince; and then come powers that could be compared to governors; rulers of the darkness of this age, which are the equivalent of legislatures; and spiritual hosts of wickedness in high places, which are the equivalent of bureaucrats who enforce the laws and write the rules. These are the ones who do most of the devil's work. They are all fallen angels who aligned themselves with Satan in rebellion against God.

Riches Revealed

Paul said that he was called to preach the unsearchable riches of Christ to the Gentiles (Eph 3:8) and to make all see the mystery that had been hidden by God so that now the manifold wisdom of God might be revealed by the church to *principalities and powers* in heavenly places (Eph 3:10). He is saying it is the responsibility of the church to let the demons know the wisdom of God in establishing his purpose through Jesus Christ (Eph 3:11).

How does the church do that? We do that by bringing in the kingdom of God. Jesus was anointed to preach the kingdom. We are saved to bring in the kingdom. In addition to that, we are to inform the demons by our activities that the kingdom of God is at hand. That happens when the church engages in prayer. We are to put on the whole armor of God so that we can pray with all kinds of prayers and supplication in the Spirit as we watch to the end with all perseverance and supplication for the saints so that the mystery of the gospel can be made known (Eph 6:18, 19).

Satan's house is raided by prayer, and the kingdom of God comes by the force of our prayer and the perseverance of our will. That is done when we pray in the Spirit and when we pray with understanding (1 Cor 14:15). What does praying in the Holy Spirit mean? Some people think that statement means to pray in tongues. Indeed that is one way to pray under the direction of the Spirit. Because that gift is not given to everyone, there must be a deeper meaning and another way.

We can learn to connect with the Spirit in prayer in ways other than praying in tongues. When we pray with understanding, we know God's will and can begin to pray it into existence. Christians should learn to pray in the Spirit. When we spend adequate time in prayer, giving thanks in all things to God, and with all perseverance, making our requests known to him, we will learn to connect with him (Phil 4:6). Our first request should be, "Lord, please teach me to pray in your Spirit."

Binding Dark Forces

When we understand that the battle is with the forces of darkness and who they are, we can pray by the Spirit to bind them, to overcome them, and to have victory over them. Satan's demons are in conflict with God's angels in heavenly places. As the book of Daniel shows us, each nation is ruled by a prince in heavenly places. The princes of darkness are in conflict with those of light. The winners are determined by our prayers. What we bind on earth is bound in heaven, and what we loose on earth is loosened in heaven (Mt 16:19).

This understanding is the key to the kingdom of heaven. We bring in the kingdom of God when we unlock the doors of heaven by what we bind on earth and what we loosen in heaven. Unfortunately, many Christians have not been taught to do that. They do not understand that they have the power and authority to bind the forces of darkness and to loosen the angels of light. For he will give his angels charge over you to protect you in all your ways (Ps 91:11), and when they are allowed to do their job, those who do his bidding will praise the Lord

(Ps 103:20-22). Due to ignorance and disbelief, the keys Christ gave us are not used.

Of course, we must believe in the demons before we can understand we have the power to bind them. It is necessary to know that evil has names and those demons can afflict our families and us. We must understand that the war for our soul is occurring continually in the heavens and that the victor is determined by our prayer. God said, "If my people who are called by my name will humble themselves, and pray and seek my face, and turn from their wicked ways, then I will hear from heaven, and will forgive their sin and heal their land" (2 Chr 7:14). We can only turn from our sin by first binding the force that causes us to sin in the first place. We cannot walk in righteousness without loosening the Holy Spirit in our life. We must not only give him permission to work in our life but also we should implore him to do so.

Before we can pray to win, we must understand that demons are not just first-century superstition, but that they are real.

Chapter 7
The Well-dressed Warrior

As a medical professional in training, I was required to wear a dress shirt and tie with casual slacks to class every day. Students were told that looking professional contributed to being professional. When we left the classroom and advanced to clinics, the attire became white smocks and blue pants. When I first moved to Oregon, I learned to recognize the hippies, loggers, and cowboys by their dress.

The large hippie population favored tie-dyed shirts and unkempt hair that needed cutting. Many of the men had beards, and the women seemed to have an aversion to shaving body parts.

The loggers wore bib overalls with flannel shirts. Their beards and hair usually needed trimming. The overalls worn by these muscular men had leather patches on the knees, for protection from the ground and the saws. Contact with the chainsaws had left grease stains on their clothes that could no longer be removed.

Cowboys were the same then as they were years before, and still are now. They wore pointed-toe boots with high heels and jeans held up by belts with large buckles, depicting a scene with a horse. The real cowboys had hats that could easily have been handed down from father to son for generations. The posers, the ones we called wannabees, had new hats that had never touched the ground nor been in the rain.

My hat had the well-worn look of one that had been around for a while. I may have grown up in Kentucky, but I had been a cowboy in my heart most of my life. I got my first pony when I was five and my last horse at fifty-five. My motto was: If I can get my leg over it, I can ride it. As a country music song reminds us, the thrill that a man who doesn't want to be thrown experiences when he throws his leg over a horse that doesn't want to be ridden cannot be expressed by words. It must be felt.

At some point in every rider's life, there is a realization that their bounce is gone and their balance is no longer good enough to ride that bucking horse without grabbing leather. When that time came in my life, I was too proud to hold on to the saddle horn and too fragile to continue plowing dirt with my face, so I gave up on horses and turned entirely to motorcycles and a different wardrobe.

People dress the part they are playing. Spandex is not a good look on me, but for bicyclists there is a purpose for that clothing. I went to a production of the *Nutcracker* ballet. The costumes were colorful and functional, but I couldn't help wondering what would inspire a grown man to put them on and jump around in front of a crowd of onlookers.

The Full Armor of God

Christians are encouraged to put on a particular type of clothing. It is not the suits and ties some wear to church on Sunday or the good dresses many women wear. It is not a pin that says I am a Christian. It is not the gold cross some hang around their neck. It is not even the Bible many carry under their arm. We are encouraged to wear the dress of a warrior. It is the whole armor of God that we should wear (Eph 6:11). Like all clothing, it has a purpose. It doesn't just identify those who are Christians, but it protects them from the wiles of the devil.

The logger's clothes protect him from the chainsaw. The clothes of a ballet dancer enable them to leap and jump in extraordinary and entertaining ways. The outfits bicyclists wear make them visible to automobiles, reduce air drag, and help them to ride further and faster than regular street clothes would. The high heels on cowboys' boots keep their feet from getting stuck in the stirrups; the hat protects them from the sun and the rain and keeps their head warm when it is cold. All functional clothing has a purpose. The same is true for the dress a Christian is intended to wear.

The Girdle of Truth

The first thing we are to put on is the girdle of truth. Ephesians 6:14 says we should put around our waist the girdle of truth before anything else. That may be more difficult than it seems at first reading. Sometimes the truth is a heavy object. Looking at what I consider the truth in someone else's life is much easier than looking at the shortcomings in my own.

I have been known to go blind to my own faults. I have failed at times to see the error of my personal motivation, even refused to look at it. I have made excuses for my failures. I have denied my fears. I have said that I would follow Jesus anywhere, yet the moment I heard his command, I ran the other direction. I have asked for opportunities to serve him and then said, not that opportunity; don't you have something else?

Before a Christian can become a warrior, they must put on the girdle of truth. This involves a sincere, honest look at oneself. After that, an in-depth look at one's belief is also required. We must ask ourselves: What is it that I believe about the Word of God? Do I think that all of it is inspired or just parts of it? What section applies to me? Do I believe the sins I wish to commit are exempt from the truth? Do I think that only some parts of the Bible refer to today? What parts of the Bible am I willing to believe? How much truth am I ready to wear?

The Breastplate of Righteousness

Once Christians have hoisted the girdle of truth around their waist, they are to put on the breastplate of righteousness (Eph 6:14). That doesn't seem so hard. Just do the right thing. However, it is not the right thing in our own eyes, but in the eyes of God that we must do. We must obey the teaching of Jesus. The word *righteousness* is a simple one. It means to do what is right. I find it interesting that Paul called it the breastplate of righteousness. The breastplate covers the chest, which contains the heart. Sin comes from the heart (Mt 15:19).

Mortal blows occur to the heart. Matthew 5:8 says that the pure in heart will see God. Proverbs 21:2 states, "Every way of a man is right in his own eyes: but the Lord pondereth the heart." The breastplate protects us from wrongdoing (Mk 7:21).

Adam and Eve should have worn one in the Garden of Eden. Because they did wrong, their hearts turned from God to Satan, and they died physically and spiritually. When we pick up the breastplate of righteousness, we have decided to walk uprightly before the Lord. If we have not made that decision, we cannot wear the breastplate. We leave ourselves open to Satan and to his mortal blows.

Shoes of Peace

The fruit of righteousness is sown in peace by those who make peace (Jas 3:18). Paul makes an assumption at this junction (Eph 6:15). He assumes the people picking up the breastplate have decided to follow Jesus. He believes they have agreed to be a part of Christ's army, under his command. Paul expects them to have put on their shoes. These shoes are the gospel of peace. These warriors are supposed to walk the path of peace. Sometimes peace can come about only as the result of a conflict, which is why Christians must wear the whole armor of God.

To walk in peace, one must understand what the gospel of peace is. Paul says the warrior is to be prepared. Warriors must know that Jesus said, "Love your enemies, bless them that curse you, do good to them that hate you and pray for them which despitefully use and persecute you" (Mt 5:44). The warrior who follows Jesus must be prepared to turn the other cheek, to forgive the trespass of others, and above all, to love as Christ has loved them.

Shield of Faith

Paul says the most important weapon of war is a defensive weapon. I would have chosen an offensive weapon such as the sword. But Paul said *above all,* take up the shield of faith so that you will be able to quench the fiery darts of the wicked one. In Paul's time, the Roman soldiers carried a large metal shield. This shield was large enough to allow the soldiers to crouch beneath it and fend off the arrows and spears hurled at them. It was strong enough to block the blow of a sword. When soldiers stood side by side, the shields made an impenetrable source of protection.

When Christians come together in prayer, their shield of faith becomes an impassable obstacle to Satan. What is the shield of faith? It is an unwavering trust in God. It is an unfailing commitment to follow Christ wherever he leads, whenever he leads, and however he leads. How big is your shield?

Helmet of Salvation and Sword of the Spirit

The next two items are the helmet of salvation and the sword of the spirit. I find it interesting that Paul has us picking them up at the same time. I wonder why he didn't say put on the helmet of salvation and then pick up the sword. It could have just been the way he worded the statement, or there could be a connection between them that I need to see.

Let us focus on the helmet of salvation first. I ride a motorcycle, and I always wear a helmet, even though Florida doesn't require one. From the time I started riding, at the age of nineteen, the states I lived in required a helmet. Now that I am in Florida, I still wear one. I feel undressed without it. A motorcycle helmet does two things. It helps protect the skull from fracture, and it protects the brain from trauma. Our brains have no attachment to the skull. In a crash, they can move within the cranium and are susceptible to bruising, which leads to concussions and bleeding. Either can be fatal.

What does the helmet of salvation offer us? Like the motorcycle helmet, it provides protection. It keeps us from stinking thinking or as we say in the south, stink-n, think-n. Like the shield of faith, the helmet of salvation also protects us from Satan's fiery darts, the darts of doubt, confusion, and the lies he tells.

When we understand salvation, Satan can't tell us we aren't saved. He can't tempt or trick us into a false gospel. We won't fall into the trap of work or good deeds and be fooled into thinking salvation is all about what we do, instead of what Jesus did on the Cross. When we know who we are in Christ, Satan can't convince us that we aren't worthy to pray to a living God. He won't be able to keep us from using the authority Christ said we should have (Mt 20:23; Jn 15:7, 16).

Christ said that whoever believed in him would do the works he did and even greater works because he was going back to the Father (Jn 14:12). If we are wearing the helmet of salvation, Satan's stink-n, think-n, will not be able to convince us otherwise. He won't be able to convince us that the promises of scripture were only meant for the apostles and that we aren't capable. We won't listen when his voice says, *why would God use you?* When he asks, *are you really a son or daughter of God,* you will say, "Yes, I am."

When we don that helmet, it is time to pick up the sword of the Spirit. When we put on the helmet of salvation, we must understand that we are saved, and we must be ready for war with the devil and prepared to walk in peace with our fellow man. When we know who we are and understand what is expected of us, what is needed from us, who equips us, and what our capabilities are, we will realize that we can indeed do all things through Christ who strengthens us (Phil 4:13). When Satan tries to tell us we aren't worthy, aren't called, aren't saved, or just aren't, we can indeed say to him, "Get thee behind me." We can speak it with authority because we wear the helmet of salvation and are wielding the sword of the spirit, which is the Word of God. The two do go hand in hand.

The sword of the Spirit is the Word of God. When we speak his Word, the demons obey, mountains move, unfruitful trees wither and die (Mt 21:21). When we speak his Word, strongholds are torn down. It is his Word on our lips that overcomes. We use that sword not to tear down other people, but to build them up.

We wield that sword to tear down strongholds of the enemy, and to make known to principalities and powers in heavenly places the manifold wisdom of God (Eph 3:10). People are not the enemy. What they do is not the enemy. The enemy is the one who makes them do what they do.

From the Closet to the Street

We war not against flesh and blood, but against powers, against rulers of the darkness of this age, and against spiritual wickedness in the heavenly places (Eph 6:12). We wage that war in our prayer closet (Mt 6:6), and from there we are to take it to the street (Mk 16:15).

Chapter 8
The Model Prayer

Imagine you have been told that you can go back in time and walk with and observe Jesus, but you cannot ask him any questions nor have any conversation with him until your last day. Then you can ask one question. What would you ask? You will see him heal the sick, rebuke demons, raise the dead, make the cripple walk, restore sight to the blind and hearing to the deaf. You will observe his habits. Daily you will see him rise before dawn and seek a place of solitude to pray. You will hear him teach and sit at his feet while you listen to his parables. You will be there when Moses and Elijah speak to him on the Mount of Transfiguration. But you will not be there when he is crucified.

Unenlightened Questions

What would your question be? The Bible records some of the questions asked of him and some concerning him. In one case, Jesus was invited to a Pharisee's home for dinner. While there, a woman known as a sinner (prostitute) came to Jesus, anointed him with oil, and with tears, sought forgiveness. When the guests saw Jesus forgive her sins, they asked among themselves, "Who is this who even forgives sins?" (Lk 7:36-49)

On one occasion, while in a ship with his disciples, a windstorm arose, and when the boat was in danger of sinking, they awakened him saying, "Master, we are perishing." After he rebuked the wind and raging water, they were afraid and said among themselves, who is this? He commands even the wind and water, and they obey him (Lk 8:22-25).

Many questions must have been asked of him. Only a few are quoted in scripture. Pilate asked Jesus if he were a king. Jarius, a ruler of the synagogue, asked and pleaded with Jesus to come to his house and heal his dying daughter (Lk 8:41). Sometimes the disciples, who should have known better, asked stupid questions of him. On his final trip to Jerusalem, Jesus and those who were with him entered a Samaritan village; instead of offering them shelter and food, the villagers turned them away. James and John, who were known as the sons of thunder, asked if he would like *for them* to call down fire from heaven to consume the village (Lk 9:51-55).

Although they had been walking with Jesus for three and one-half years, from this question, it is apparent his teaching had made little impact on them. It would seem they were only interested in the power he could give them. I have known some Christians like that. Some who have walked with Christ for years without understanding his teaching only wanted to demonstrate his power for their recognition. They lacked love and compassion and had lost sight of the reason for that power.

A Believer's Question

I think the most intelligent question asked of Jesus came from the disciple who asked him to teach them to pray (Lk 11:1). The Bible doesn't say who that was. It may have been someone other than one of the twelve apostles. At one time, Jesus had as many as seventy disciples following him (Mk 13:14).

The Lord's Prayer, as many call it—or the model prayer, as some refer to it—should be construed as a guide for prayer, not just seen as a prayer to be recited. It teaches us a method for dressing in the whole armor of God. I have heard many teach on the armor of God, but I have never heard anyone say how we are to put on that armor. I hope to explain that now. Let us look at this prayer (Mt 6:8-13).

> *Our Father which art in heaven, Hallowed be thy name.*
> *Thy kingdom come, thy will be done on earth, as it is in heaven.*
> *Give us this day our daily bread.*
> *And forgive us our debts as we forgive our debtors.*
> *Lead us not into temptation, but deliver us from evil.*
> *For thine is the kingdom, the power, and the glory forever,*
> *Amen.*

Paul taught us to begin our dress from the feet up. Jesus starts from the head down.

In an earlier chapter, I encouraged you to spend an hour in prayer. Using this prayer as a guide, divide your prayer time into four segments. The first fifteen minutes should be in thanksgiving for what God has done, and praise to the Father for who he is. The second fifteen minutes should be in praying for the kingdom to come into your life so that his will can be done. That includes praying for forgiveness of your sins and to forgive others for theirs. It is also a time to thank him for meeting your daily needs. The third part is a time of intercession. In this time of prayer defeat the devil in your life and in the lives of others. The fourth part is a declaration of who God is and what you believe. Now let us look at this prayer in greater depth.

Paul said that we should wear the helmet of salvation. Christ taught that our prayer should begin with, "Our Father who art in heaven." Those wearing the helmet of salvation must know they are saved. If they don't, Satan will cast doubt into their mind, and like Goliath, the smallest of pebbles will take them to their knees.

Our Father

One of the problems some have with this beginning is the term "Our Father." Instinctively, when we use the word, *Father,* our minds go back to our own fathers. Even when we try not to, our minds compare God to the father we had.

Some children see their fathers as dictators and tyrants. That can cause them to see God only as someone who makes rules, having no exceptions. If so, they will not see him as a God of mercy. Those whose father criticized everything they did will think of God as a judge. If their father were stern and demanding, they would expect God to be also. Those, who were given approval only as a result of their performance, would feel the need to perform for God—not because of their love for him, but because they think it's the only way he will love them. Because they work for the wrong reason, they will never consider themselves approved. To some extent, all religions exploit this and use it to keep people in bondage.

Children whose fathers were poor providers may not expect anything from God. Conversely, if their father gave them everything they asked for and required nothing of them, they may regard God as a candy store and nothing more. They may only come to him when they want something.

When we begin this prayer, there is no room for stink-n think-n. We must understand that our Father in heaven is different from our father on earth. His ways are higher than ours; his thoughts are higher than ours (Is 55:9). He knows our needs before we ask (Mt 6:8). If our earthly father knows how to give us good things, how much more will our heavenly Father give to those who ask him (Mt 7:11).

The Father's Love

God does not want to be our judge. We do not need to fear to come before him. Paul said, "Let us come boldly before the throne of grace that we might obtain mercy and grace to help in the time of need (Heb 4:16). He said that if we judged ourselves, we would not be judged (1 Cor 11:31).

If we understood the love God has for us, we wouldn't fear him. We would cling to him, and we would realize how precious we are in his sight. Paul prayed that Christ might dwell in our hearts through faith and because of that we might be rooted and grounded in love. He prayed that we would be able to comprehend what are the width and length and depth and height of that love. He said that knowing the love of Christ fills us with all the fullness of God (Eph 3:14-19). If Christians could understand the magnitude of Christ's love, if they felt

God's love in their hearts, their lives would be forever changed.

I once asked myself these questions; perhaps they will be of help to you:

Why, Lord, do I think you love others, but not necessarily me? What is the width, length, depth, and height of your love for me?

Lord, how deep is your love? Is it as deep as the sea? What is that depth? Does your love extend into space? Is there enough to encompass the universe? How much love is that?

How wide is your love? Is it wide enough to go around the world? How much does that require? Will it cover the world in all directions at the same time?

How high is your love? Does it reach the top of my head or just to the bottoms of my feet? Does it stop somewhere in between? Does it go to the top of the tallest mountain or only to the foothills?

If the world were placed in a box, how big would the box be? Would the container be large enough to require packing? Would your love be the packing? Would there be enough love to protect the content? How far would you go to protect your creation?

How much love, God, do you have? Is it enough to encircle me and everyone like me, or does it encompass only a few? Do you love every person in the world or just some of them? Do you love just the pretty people or is your love blind?

Do you love just the good people, or does it cover a sinner like me? Is your love conditional, or do you love me and those like me no matter what? Does it include me when I am naughty or just when I am nice? How bad must I be before you quit loving me?

If you like me when I behave, would you love me if I were better? If I am really good, how much would you love me? How much good is enough?

Do you have enough love to include the animals? They can't worship you. They don't bow down to you. I suspect they don't disobey you either. You must love animals. You created them before you created man. You asked Jonah to consider them. You wanted to know if Jonah would have you destroy them along with the Ninivites.

Do you love birds? You must. Jesus said they neither plant nor store up in barns, yet you provide for them.

Do you love the lilies of the field? How much love does a flower need? Jesus said you clothe them. My wife says they need complimenting. She says flowers do better if you talk to them. I like and appreciate the high mountain flowers that bloom in the spring. Their colors bless me. They inspire me to give thanks to you. How much do you love the lilies of the field?

A farmer cares for his fields and watches over his crops. Does that mean he loves them? A shepherd will risk his own life for his sheep. Does he love them?

How much love do you have, God? Is it enough to cover the world and everything in it? Does that love cover just people, or does it include the animals, the birds of the air, and the fish of the sea? Does it cover plants as well?

How much love does it take to cover everything you created? How much is needed to protect, nurture, and nourish all that you have made?

Do you cry when a bird falls from the sky or when a dog dies? Does a tree feel the pain of the ax, and do you feel the pain of the tree? Do you cry over me?

How much love, Lord, do you have? Will it run out or will it last forever? Do you have more love some days than others? Is there a meter on your well of love? How deep is that well? How much love does it contain?

How much love does it take God for you to care about everything you have made? How far are you willing to go to show that love? Are you ready to answer my prayers? Are you willing to live in me? Will you spend time with me? Will you care for me when I am sick, ugly, or just plain mean? When will you love me?

Father, how wide, deep, and long is your love? How can I measure your love for me, let alone for others? How can I comprehend your love for the entire world? How far does your love go?

I know, you so loved your creation that you sacrificed your only son so that no part of it need perish so that it could all be saved. You understood that mankind is the only part of your creation with the capacity to destroy everything that you made. That is why you sent your most precious son. He would show the way. He is the way.

How can I know the magnitude of your love? I can't measure it. Even if I could, I couldn't comprehend the size of the box that holds it. How can I know how much you love me?

I know, all I must do is look to the hill called Golgotha. The Cross my Lord died upon is all the love I need to see. How does one measure the love that was enough to cause someone to die for them? How much love was required? It must have been all the love they had. That, Lord, must be the amount of love you have for me.

With Thanksgiving

When I understand the magnitude of Christ's love for me, I am filled with the fullness of God (Eph 3:14-10). I know what he did because of it, and I know that a God who loves me that much hears and answers my prayers. Satan can't convince me otherwise. I have not only put on the helmet of salvation, but I am ready to pray in all things with thanksgiving.

We are to enter his gates with thanksgiving and come into the court of heaven with praise, blessing his name (Ps 100:4). That is not difficult when we grasp the magnitude of his love for us. When we understand that his kingdom brings peace and joy into our life by righteousness, it is easy to pray for his will to be done. The peace of God which surpasses all understanding will guard our hearts and minds through Jesus Christ because we pray about all things with supplication and thanksgiving (Phil 4:6-7).

I do not want to convey that there is only one way to pray, but I do want to encourage everyone who prays to learn to pray with thanksgiving. The way we express things can negate the effectiveness of our prayers. The things we don't pray for will not be given to us. I am going to explain what I mean as we look at the rest of this model prayer.

Luke chapter 11:9-10 encourages us to ask, seek, knock, and find. That is what we do in prayer. Jesus said that everyone who asks receives; he who seeks will find; and to him who knocks, it will be opened. In prayer, we ask, seek, and knock. The ways we go about it make a difference. If we don't ask, we won't receive; if we don't seek, we won't find; and if we don't knock on the doors of heaven, they won't open.

When we understand who the Father is, praying with thanksgiving for what he has done is not difficult. When we know he is in heaven, praying with praise is possible. Remember we praise God for who he is; we thank him for what he has done, is doing, and is going to do.

When we pray for the kingdom to come, what is it that we are asking for? We are seeking power to live peacefully, to have the peace that passes all understanding (Phil 4:7). We are asking for the ability to do what Jesus did, and even more (Mk 16:17). We are knocking on the doors of heaven so that we might know the will of God. When his kingdom comes, his will is done (Mt 6:10). When it happens, we have put on the breastplate of righteousness.

When we understand the love of Christ—which is all the fullness of God—instead of begging for our daily bread, we can thank him for our food. If your child came and said, "Thank you for the lunch money you are giving me today," would you ask, "How much do you need," or would you say, "Why should I give you anything?" Would you make them beg?

When we understand the love of God and comprehend the inner peace that comes from living in his kingdom, we can go to him in thanksgiving for all things, because we are anxious for nothing (Mt 6:25-33). When we understand that he provides for the birds of the air, the fish in the sea, and clothes the lilies of the field; and when we grasp that we are his most precious creation, it should be easy to believe that he will provide for our needs that he already knows we have (Mt 6:8).

Forgive Us Our Debts

The next part of this prayer may be the most difficult for some. Forgive us our debts as we forgive our debtors, or as some versions of the Bible say, forgive our sins as we forgive those who sin against us. I frequently hear Christians asking questions. These are the two I hear most often: "How can I hear the Lord speaking to me?" and "Why is it so hard to forgive?" We should also ask this question: "Why it is so important to forgive?"

Remember that, in this prayer, we have asked for God's kingdom to come and for his will to be done. In respect to forgiveness, what does that mean? God's kingdom, like all kingdoms, is one of laws. Jesus said, "Judge not lest you be judged. With the measure you use, it will be measured back to you" (Mt 7:1-2). Because God's kingdom is one of peace and power within us, we cannot live in his kingdom when sin stands in the way.

We want God to forgive our sins. He cannot and will not do that if we will not let go of those perpetrated against us. When we hold on to those sins, we are holding on to the kingdom of Satan and not the kingdom of God.

When we keep hate, which is the opposite of love, it blocks the power of the Holy Spirit to work in our life. It grieves the Holy Spirit, which we are told not to do (Eph 4:30). Remember, the sons of God are those who obey God.

Once we have confessed our sins to God, both the sins which we know we are guilty of and those that remain hidden in our hearts, we must ask forgiveness for them and ask him to help us forgive those to whom we harbor ill will. Forgiveness is an act of God's grace. We are forgiven by grace, and we must have the grace to forgive. In a later chapter, I am going to show how to pray for forgiveness.

Once we have conquered forgiveness and understood how it works, we can be assured that the next part of our prayer will be answered. At this point, around our waist we wear the girdle of truth, we have put on the breastplate of righteousness and the shoes of peace, we have put on the helmet of salvation, and now we are ready to pick up the shield of faith.

Lead Us Not

When we ask not to be led into temptation but to be delivered from the evil one, we should do so with thanksgiving and not trepidation. It is the sins in our life that put a barrier between God and us. Sometimes God must allow that sin to take place before we can see its depth in our heart.

Evil enters through the eye (Mt 6:23), but sin comes from the heart. When saying thank you, Father, for delivering me from evil, be sure to confess the evil to which you are referring. The temptations that plague us are not sins, but yielding to them is. Satan will lay claim to the sins we harbor and will ask to try us. Remember Job. He was a man whom God considered righteous, yet Satan was allowed to test him (Jb 1:1, 12).

Thy Kingdom Come

When we pray for the kingdom to come, we are asking for the power of God to establish righteousness in our heart and to protect us from evil. We are expecting to have authority to wield the sword of the spirit, which is the Word of God. Using that sword, we can bind the strong man, rob his house, and lay claim to the will of God in our lives and in the lives of others.

When we have determined the will of God, we can wield the sword of the Spirit effectively. When we pray his will, he will hear us, and Jesus will do as we have asked (Jn 14:13, 14). After we have repented of the sins to which we have confessed, the kingdom of God comes because God has heard our prayer (Jn 9:31).

Go Forth

When we have girded our loins in truth, put on the breastplate of righteousness, taken hold of the shield of faith, are holding the sword of the spirit in our hand, and are wearing the helmet of salvation, the will of God can be manifested through us and to us. It is now time to go forth, shod in the gospel of peace; it is time to take God's will, his Word, and his grace to our world so that he can use us as he wills to do the things Jesus did.

As *he* did, *we* will now be able to do—to give the knowledge of salvation to the lost, to provide light to those who sit in the shadow of darkness (sin) and the shadow of death, to know his will, to do his will, and to allow him to guide our feet in the way of peace (Lk 1:77-79).

The next chapters will give examples and explain how to apply this teaching.

Chapter 9
Praying for Forgiveness

What is the most challenging part of your Christian walk? What do you struggle with the most? If you said forgiveness, you would have a lot of company. I have heard many Christians ask this question: Why it is so hard to forgive? Have you ever been angry at someone, with whom you didn't live, and after struggling in prayer, thought that you had forgiven them. Then one day you see them on the street, and suddenly you experience those old feelings of anger as though their slight had just happened? Most of us have had that experience.

Vengeance is Whose?

I used to prefer getting even to forgiveness. I could forgive that person after I had gotten even with them. With patience, I would wait months, or even years, to do to them what they had done to me. Give them time to forget and let their guard down, then strike the blow of retribution. Have any of you had those feelings or done that? I could think of the most ingenious ways to exact my vengeance.

When the Holy Spirit convicted me of my unforgiveness, I would pray and think that I had forgiven, and then I would avoid the objects of my wrath. Better to cut them off than to be exposed to them. After all, they might do the same thing again. That wasn't forgiveness, and it would become apparent when at the most unexpected moment, I would see them and the old feelings and the desire for revenge would swell up within me. Why, God, can't I forgive them? What must I do to let it go?

Kindness as a Remedy?

When I hear Christians ask why forgiveness is so difficult, I have an answer. It is a simple one. I say, "You don't understand." I have heard well-meaning preachers teach on forgiveness, sometimes in multiple sermons, explaining in detail every problem caused by unforgiveness. I have listened to them encourage acts of kindness as the means of letting go. Acts of kindness may indeed prevent you from getting even any time soon, but they will not keep you from wanting retribution. Kind acts won't get someone to apologize for what may have been done to you. That person may not realize their actions have offended you. They may not care. In any case, a good deed on your part, without the proper motivation, will have no effect on your feelings. It will just make you seem more self-righteous in your own eyes and possibly in the eyes of others as well.

How Do You See God?

The way we view God affects our ability to forgive. How do you see God? If you see God as a taskmaster demanding you work for every reward, you will expect the same from someone who offends you. If you see him as a judge, you expect him to act like one.

Judges are supposed to get justice for victims of injustice. Their job is to get revenge for those who won't do it for themselves. Whoa! That statement is incorrect. Their job is to get justice for those who can't do it for themselves. Is justice what someone who lost a child to a killer wants? If it were your child, would you consider life in prison—with television, three meals a day and free medical care—as justice? Or would you want for them the death penalty they deserved?

Justice is complex. Sometimes it is no more than restitution. Have you prayed that God would make someone pay you the money they owed? Have you asked him to make them sorry for the hurt they have caused? These are the things expected from a judge. Justice is accomplished when the offending party pays for their misdeeds. A judge is required to see that they do.

Those who can't forgive or who have difficulty forgiving see God as a judge and expect him to act like one. They want and expect retribution. If they can't get it, they harbor ill will in their heart and allow it to fester. Unforgiveness is like cancer.

Cut It Out

Cancer has many causes, but most of them are the result of exposure to chemicals—chemicals we eat, breathe, touch, or those injected into us in the form of drugs.

The process is complex. Some gene within our body allows that chemical to begin a process which causes one cell to mutate. Soon that mutated cell becomes two mutated cells, then four, and in a short time sixteen. They form a small mass invisible to the naked eye and undetected by its victim. With a little more time it is a tiny lump that is seemingly causing no harm, but as time goes by, its damage becomes noticeable. Soon some cells break from that lump and start a new lump somewhere else. As those lumps grow, they take over the organ they are found in and kill the very tissue supporting them.

Unforgiveness is like that. It starts with a small slight, which grows into a lump. Then an unforgiving person spreads it with his/her tongue to others. It is called slander. Sometimes it is the result of jealousy caused by our own avarice, but many times it is the result of our desire for revenge or our need for vindication. We want our actions to be justified in our own mind.

When possible, the best treatment for cancer is a sharp knife, a wide incision, and a deep cut, done quickly. Cutting that cancer out before it spreads increases the chance for survival. Forgiving entirely and quickly is our best chance of recovery. Don't let the sun set on your anger, because hate will greet the dawn.

The Way to Forgiveness

OK, how do we forgive? Everything said so far may be true, but it hasn't done anything to help us forgive. The first thing we must do is change the way we look at God. People who see God as a judge expect him to judge them for their sins, and they want others to be judged. People who don't understand grace expect to pay for their sins, and they intend for others to do the same.

We Sinners

On most Sundays the preacher tells us what sinners we are, what level of sin we have committed, and what punishment we deserve. Religion capitalizes on our guilt. It holds us in bondage. Instead of teaching us to be saints, whom the Bible says we become when Jesus is our Lord, religion is continually reminding us that we are sinners.

In that way, we are unknowingly taught that we haven't been forgiven. We are encouraged to work for that forgiveness by putting more in the offering and doing more in the church, and we are left feeling guilty because we aren't doing enough.

Saved By Grace

Many in the pulpits and the pews are missing one thing: they neither understand nor appreciate God's grace. It is a proper understanding of his grace that makes forgiveness possible. In fact, it is the only thing that makes it possible. I have never met a Christian who couldn't quote the definition of grace. They are quick to express that it is God's unmerited favor. The problem is that very few understand what that definition stems from, and even fewer have experienced it in their own hearts.

Grace is an act of love. It is the result of God's love. We must experience it in our own hearts before we can give it to others. Instead of being told that we are sinners, we should be taught to be filled with the love of Christ so that we might be filled with all the fullness of God. What is God full of (Eph 3:19)?

God is love. God is nothing but love, and we should be encouraged to become rooted and grounded in the magnitude of that truth (1 Jn 4:16). We must experience his love in our hearts so that we can be filled with all the fullness of God (Eph 3:17-19). God is full of love, and we need to know and understand that truth from experience.

Paul taught that love is all the things that lead to forgiveness. It is patient and kind, it doesn't envy, doesn't show off, is not full of itself, doesn't behave rudely. It is not easily provoked, doesn't rejoice in iniquity, but does rejoice in the truth. It bears all things, believes all things, endures all things and never fails (1 Cor 13:4-8).

When I felt, for myself, God's love for me and everyone like me, I understood for the first time the meaning of grace. Grace is love. There is nothing more than that. It is the fullness of God. When we experience his love in our own heart, forgiveness is easy.

When I find that I am angry with someone, and when I discover that I am accusing and judging them, I go to my knees in prayer. I don't pray about the situation or the other person. Instead, I judge myself by looking at the problems in my own heart, those which may cause me to accuse someone else. I confess those to the Lord.

When an injustice has been done to me, I pray. I don't ask to forgive the hurt. I don't seek justice. I don't try to overlook the misdeed. I don't pray about it at all. *I ask the Lord to give me his supernatural love for that person.*

Love always forgives. I am amazed at how quickly my anger dissipates. Soon I am praying for their well-being, and I'm asking God to bless them and to help them discover his love for themselves. I no longer remember their trespass.

When I ask him to forgive them their trespasses as he has excused mine, his kingdom has come. The next time I see them, instead of anger welling up inside of me, I demonstrate that I have compassion, and instead of trying to avoid them, I reach out to them. Because I genuinely care for them, I have forgotten their sin, just as the Lord has forgotten mine. I no longer need to turn the other cheek.

Next to Jesus dying on the Cross for our sin, one of the best examples of God's grace is the story of the woman caught in adultery. The pastors and teachers of the temple threw at Jesus' feet a helpless woman caught in the act of adultery. They wanted him to pronounce judgment upon her. They recited the law and asked if he agreed with it. They saw the law as an excuse for punishment. They weren't willing to forgive, they weren't looking for justice. They had already judged her by their accusations. They wanted a sentence carried out (Jn 8:3-11).

It was now time for them to be judged. As you judge, so will you also be judged (Mt 7:1, 2). The Bible says that Jesus stopped and wrote something in the ground. Many speculate on what that may have been. I believe that he wrote "Deuteronomy 5" in the soil. Each of these men would know that this contained the words that God spoke to all of the children of Israel.

They knew that he spoke them with a loud voice to those assembled at the mountain from the midst of the fire, the cloud, and the thick darkness. They knew he had written them on two stones and had given those to Moses. They knew the entire content of these Ten Commandments upon which the Mosaic Law was based. As youths, they had memorized these verses and could quote them from memory.

When Jesus said, "Let him among you who is without sin throw the first stone," each of them stood convicted in their hearts of their own sins, and each, in turn, walked away. When Jesus asked the woman who judged her, she looked around and said, "No one." He replied, "Neither do I." That is God's grace. It is letting go of judgment.

In ancient times when the king made a decree and signed it, he was as obligated to live up to the law, as were his subjects. I have previously stated that forgiveness is a law of God's kingdom. Jesus said that when we are praying if we have anything against someone, we are to forgive them so that God may forgive us. It is easy to interpret that as *may be willing*, but that is not what it means. It means so that God *may be able* to forgive us. In the very next breath, Jesus said that if you do not forgive, neither will your father in heaven forgive your sins. Forgiveness is a law of the kingdom. God cannot forgive us if we don't forgive others (Mk 11:25, 26).

Every Christian must comprehend who the Father in heaven is and understand that he is love. Once you have felt the love, the compassion God has for you and everyone else, giving his love to others will not be difficult. When you know just how much he cares for you, you will no longer feel the need to work for his approval. When you comprehend grace, that understanding will enable you to extend grace to others in the same way. God's love in you will allow you to forgive.

First Is Love

I have heard some teach that one must do good deeds to forgive, and others explain that you must forgive in order to love. I say, *you must first love so that you can forgive and can perform good deeds.*

Chapter 10
Thy Will Be Done

The two questions I most often hear Christians ask are "How do I hear God?" and "How do I know his will?" Pastors usually say to look in the Word. Most people asking those questions are hoping for a different answer, and I have one: learn to pray! It is in prayer that I hear his voice and through prayer that I discover his will. Sometimes he tells me to look in the Bible, and at times he has given me the chapter and verse. At other times, I have just opened the book, and my eyes have fallen on the verse that gave me the answer. Sometimes he tells me his will, either by speaking to me or in the way he directs my prayer.

His Voice

One time when I was praying, the Lord interrupted my thoughts and said, "Don't buy the property you are looking at. I have something else in mind for you." The sudden sound of his voice caught me off guard. I was especially surprised by his knowledge of my intention. I had not discussed it with him. At that moment, I felt the need for confirmation. Was God speaking to me?

I said, "Lord would you mind confirming that?" He told me to look in my Bible at a specific book, chapter, and verse. I then asked which version of the Bible. I owned more than one version and knew that each of them had slight differences. I heard him say, "King James." When I opened to that verse, the words that greeted me said: Stay where you are, look unto the fields. I wish I remembered the location of that verse, but I do not. In that situation, the Bible had the answer, but my prayer led me to it. To this day the King James Version is my favorite.

His Word

Of course, most of the time, we aren't fortunate enough to hear him so clearly. A few years ago, I was in terrible pain from a medical condition and was praying for healing, when I felt compelled to open the Bible in front of me. I randomly opened to a verse in the Old Testament that said, I will not heal your land. I took it to mean that he was not going to cure me of my medical problem. I had also been praying about the condition of our country at the same time, and I wasn't sure how to apply the answer.

Because I am a trained scientist, I also wondered if this was a coincidence, instead of an attempt on God's part to communicate with me. The next six times I opened that Bible, it was to the same page and verse. As soon as I accepted it as God's Word to me, I could not open it to that page again, even though I tried.

I continued in prayer, still not sure of his will. If he wasn't going to heal me, there was nothing I could do to change his mind. So I gave thanks to him for the way he intended to deal with my health. I praised him for his outcome. I thanked him for the lesson I would learn from the experience and the good that would come from it.

Fortunately, I was able to manage the pain and the discomfort until the Lord revealed the source of my problem. I was having a severe reaction to a statin drug my cardiologist prescribed. After visiting four different specialists and being told by each of them that the statin drug wasn't the problem, I finally called my cardiologist and was told to quit the drug immediately. Within three months I was better, and after three years I no longer had any remaining issues.

Sometimes Christians seek help for spiritual problems from the wrong doctors. Unless their counselors have a relationship with the Holy Spirit, their diagnosis may be like the ones given to me by the doctors I saw—wrong. Spiritual problems need treating spiritually. That can only be done through prayer, allowing the Holy Spirit access to the innermost parts of our heart. It is God's will to heal; it is our responsibility to let him.

His Will

One time in prayer, I mentioned that there was something I needed to do for Jesus but that I didn't know what it was. All of my Christian life, I have felt that I had a specific purpose, but I had never understood what it was. At that moment I heard God say, "I have already shown you what I want, you just don't see it." I agreed with him.

I said, "You are right, I don't. You are going to need to shout or do something else if you expect me to know what it is. I just don't see it." I wish I could say that I heard him tell me what it was, but I didn't. I did hear myself say, "Unless it is those three books rattling around in my head." When I said that, a light came on, and I understood what he wanted.

Understanding God's will in some situations can be complicated. But most of the time we already have the answer. Understanding the nature of God's kingdom helps to simplify the process. In the Lord's Prayer, the model prayer, we are taught to say *Thy kingdom come, thy will be done*. Notice the relationship! First, the kingdom comes, then the will. Look at what happens next! *Give us this day our daily bread*, followed by, *And forgive us our debts as we forgive our debtors*.

Seek First the Kingdom

Each step leads to the next. We must first enter the kingdom of God if we are going to receive his blessing. After repenting of our sin, inviting Jesus to be our Lord, and accepting the Holy Spirit as our guide, companion, teacher and strength, we are entitled to live in the kingdom and to receive its benefits. To enter into that kingdom, we must live righteously. That doesn't mean being perfect, but it means to do what is right. What is that? It is to love the Lord our God with all our heart, soul, and mind and our neighbor as ourselves (Lk10:27). It is to put on the whole armor of God daily and walk with him. When we do these things, we are living in the kingdom and are entitled to all of its provisions. This leads to peace in our hearts and joy in our lives.

What did Jesus say? He said, "Why do you worry?" What is it that we worry about? We worry about our next meal, the clothes we wear, the house we live in, the money we need, the family we have. Every other worry is a subset of those things. Jesus said that if God can feed the birds of the air and clothe the lilies of the field and the grass, then why do you worry? If he can do that for them, how much more will he do for you? He already knows the things we need. How do we get them? We seek first the kingdom of God and then all these things will be provided (Mt 6:25-33).

Doing Our Part

We must understand and believe that he is not like our earthly father. He has a greater capacity. He loves us more, he cares more, and his resources are more abundant. He has the will and the power to provide (Mt 7:11). No matter how much our earthly father wants for us, God wants more.

Understanding that, how then should we pray? Instead of continually pleading with him for things, thank him for the way he is going to provide. Instead of begging for enough money to get through the week, thank him for showing you how to manage the money you have and for favor with your creditors.

Remember his challenge to all of us: He tells us to "Bring ye all the tithes into the storehouse, that there may be meat in mine house, and prove me now herewith, saith the LORD of hosts, if I will not open you the windows of heaven, and pour you out a blessing, *that there shall not be room enough to receive it.* And I will *rebuke the devourer* for your sakes" (Mal 3:10-11). He will not be able to destroy the fruit of your field nor the labor of your hand (my paraphrase). He did not say give me a thousand dollars, and I will return one hundred ten thousand, and you won't have to do any work for it.

Who is the enemy of our success? We are if we don't seek first the kingdom of God and his righteousness. Who is behind our failure to succeed—Satan himself. He will tempt us to ask from the lusts of our heart. The Bible says that we have not because we ask amiss (Jas 4:3). We pray to satisfy our desires instead of seeking God's kingdom. Who can turn that around? What is your part in that?

Repentance Before Prayer

In addition to giving us our daily bread, what else is God's will for us? He wants to forgive our sins. "Forgive us our sins as we forgive the sins of others" (Mt 6:12). I have heard it said that confession is good for the soul. The person who doesn't ask for forgiveness is hesitant to approach God. The more forgiveness we need, the more substantial the burden we carry. Eventually, when the load becomes unbearable, that soul and the person it inhabits collapses under the weight of their sin, and one of two things happens, either Satan takes over their life or they surrender it to God. Christians don't have to bear the burden of guilt, though some still do so.

Jesus said that not everyone who says Lord, Lord shall enter the kingdom of heaven. Only those who do the will of the Father shall (Mt 7:21). Only those who obey God will enter his kingdom in heaven, and only those who repent and follow the Holy Spirit will live in his kingdom on earth (Mt 4:17).

We know that God answers not the prayers of sinners, but if anyone is a worshiper of God and does his will, that one he hears (Jn 9:31). It is God's will for us to confess and to repent. The righteous person is the one who confesses and repents of sin. The unrighteous bear guilt. The righteous person is not a perfect person, but merely someone who puts God first. Righteous people understand that they sin, and they confess their sins to the God of Grace who is willing and able to forgive.

Seek His Will

How do I know that I am in God's will? Remember the kingdom is righteousness, peace, and joy within us. When I am seeking God's will, I do so in prayer, and I continue in prayer until he gives me an answer. When I receive that answer, I have peace in my spirit. If I get an answer that does not come with peace, I continue to pray. Either the answer did not come from God or I did not understand what he was saying to me or I didn't want to hear the answer he gave.

One guideline I use in interpreting God's voice is that if something sounds too good to be true, it probably came from Satan. If it contradicts the principles of scripture, it definitely came from Satan. If it is something I want to do, it is me. If it is something I don't want to do but know in my spirit God does, I may wrestle with him and even plead, but in the end, I take up my cross and follow him.

Resolve to Win

Once we determine God's will, our job is only partly done. Now *it is our responsibility to pray it to completion.* Just knowing God's will is no guarantee that it will be done. Satan will do all in his power to keep that from happening. Because the God in us is stronger than the one afflicting us, we can overcome by prayer and resolve. Wearing the full armor of God, go to your knees and wage war to win.

Chapter 11
Lead and Deliver

Jesus draws us to a conclusion in this model prayer with the statement, "Lead us not into temptation but deliver us from evil." (Mt 6:13). The first two words that speak to me in this are *lead* and *deliver*. The second two are *temptation* and *evil*. Each of these paired words speaks to the understanding we must have if we are going to have victory over the enemy.

It is necessary to understand temptation from God's perspective. Temptation is not sin; it is the prelude to sin. It is what entices us to sin. Sin results when temptation is taken into our hearts and allowed to have its way with us (Jas 1:14, 15). Everyone is tempted at one time or another. Even Jesus was tempted. In Matthew chapter 4, Jesus was led into the wilderness to be tempted of Satan after he was baptized with the Holy Spirit. There he was tempted to doubt his ancestry. Was he really the son of God?

He was challenged to prove his heritage by turning rock into bread and also to prove it by throwing himself from the temple roof. When Satan couldn't lead Jesus to sin in those ways, he acknowledged his heritage and mission and tempted Jesus to take a shortcut to achieve his purpose. Once again, Jesus resisted and Satan left him alone for a season.

Tempting God

Every Christian is tempted in those same ways. As a child of God, do you believe he can provide for your needs? Do you feel the need to turn your own rock into bread, or do you think that he will provide if you seek first the kingdom of God? Do you need proof that you are a child of God? Do you need to test him? Do you claim a promise from scripture made to only one person and demand that God fulfills it for you? Do you think refusing to seek medical help while claiming healing through faith will please him enough to get you the healing? Do you require that healing as proof God loves you? Are you tempting God?

I saw two different families in Oregon do that. In one case the parents refused help for their diabetic child while believing in faith for God's healing; and another refused to take their child, with a ruptured appendix, to the hospital because they were praying for God to provide healing. In both cases, the child died, and the parents went to jail. In each case, the parents belonged to a religious group that believed healing was a test of faith. They did not understand that a test of faith does not involve tempting God.

Have you tried to bargain with God? Have you promised him something if he would do something for you? That is another form of tempting God. Rejoice that he did not agree to the deal, lest you be required to hold up your end of the bargain.

Has God given you a job? Did you fulfill it to his specifications or did you take a shortcut? You say God has never given you a job. If you are a Christian, he has. Do you love your neighbor as yourself? Do you pray for those who spitefully use you? How often?

Resisting Temptation

The Bible says that Jesus was tempted in every way we are, but he was without sin (Heb 4:15). Do you have feelings of lust, greed, or anger?

Do you ever have the desire to say, "not your will God but mine?" Are you tempted by gluttony in any form? In how many ways are you tempted? The Bible says that Jesus was tempted in every way, yet he was without sin (Heb 4:15). Because he understands how we are tempted, he knows how to help us with temptations (Heb 2:18).

Temptations of the Flesh

We face two types of temptations. The first temptation is the lure of the flesh. The devil is like a roaring lion; walking about looking for those he may devour (1 Pet 5:8). He is like the fisherman. First, he baits the hook and then throws it out to see who will bite. The temptation could come in the form of a pretty woman or a handsome man. He may appeal to our greed or to our jealousy. An angry person is easy prey. Anger results in murder, either in the heart or in deed. A gluttonous person is a greedy person. They can never get enough. Whether it is money, attention, sex or possessions, they never have enough. A jealous person practices deceit and division while causing dissension. These are all the things that Satan does.

The Test of Temptations

The second type of temptation is a test of our faith. The devil is allowed to try our faith so that God may know the depth of our love for him (Dt 13:3). This type of test is painful and sometimes lengthy. It is a process of refining. This testing refines our faith much as fire does gold. It burns away the impurities and purifies our faith so that in the end we receive the salvation of our souls (1 Pt 1:6-8).

This test requires Satan to get permission to try the person. When Christians yield to the sins of the flesh, there is no need for a test of faith. Those who have laid aside the sins of the flesh, to please God, will be further purified by the testing of their faith. Jesus told Peter that Satan has desired to sift him as wheat but said that he had prayed his faith would not fail (Lk 22:31).

The best example of this is the story of Job. Job was upright and blameless; he shunned evil and feared God (Jb 1:1). He was a rich man. He had sons and daughters and many cattle and sheep. He was a caring father. He made sacrifices to God for his children, in case they had sinned with one another or cursed God in their hearts (Jb 1:1-5).

The Bible says that on a day when the sons of God (angels) came before him, Satan was among them. God asked where he had been. Satan said he was going to and fro on the earth. God, knowing that he was looking for those whom he could devour, asked if he had considered his servant Job? That is, have you tested him (Jb 1:6-8)?

Satan replied that he could not because God had placed a hedge of thorns around him. He then incited God to allow him to be tested (Jb 1:9, 10), and God gave him permission. The rest of the story is one of loss and struggle, but in the end it is one of redemption and victory. Satan had to get God's permission for each and every test. Job had to stand up or fall.

Why did God allow Job to be tested as he was? He lost everything that he had: his family, his wealth, and his health. I personally think it was for two reasons: one, to prove a point to Satan; and two, to refine a perfect faith in Job. The Bible says God allows Satan to try us in order to know all that is in our heart, as he did with Hezekiah who, by the way, failed the test (2 Chr 32:30, 31). I continually pray that God will not bet on me. I am no Job. I just hope that he doesn't decide to prove that I am.

Made Better

There is no sin in temptation; indeed the Bible says that we should count it all as joy because it is a testing of our faith (Jas 1:2-3). It states that we are taught patience through the test, and when we allow it to run its course, we will be perfected and wanting in nothing. Blessed is the man that endures temptation, for he shall receive the crown of life that Jesus promised to them that love him (Jas 1:4, 12). Of course, that promise is based upon successfully completing the test. If we fail, we may get to repeat it.

I don't like to be tested. I don't know anyone who does. From the tests of my faith, I have learned to be patient and wait upon the Lord. They only last for a season (1 Pt 1:6). They have taught me the depth of my convictions and shown to me the extent of my trust in the Lord. Because of them, I have discovered my own weakness.

From each trial and temptation in my life, I have been made a better man. At the beginning of my refining, I caved to the lusts of the flesh and went through the tests of faith, kicking and screaming. Gradually, I learned to look for the silver lining and to remember that all things work together for good to those who love the Lord, and who are called according to his purpose (Rom 8:28).

I believe and know from experience that God is faithful and will not allow me to be tested beyond my capabilities. I know he will enable me to bear it and will make a means of escape (1 Cor 10:13).

If temptation is such a rewarding thing, why then did Jesus say we should pray to avoid it? When we pray "lead us not into temptation," we must understand that it is not God who leads, but our own lust. God cannot be tempted with evil, neither does he tempt any man (Jas 1:13, 14). Satan does that.

Jesus wants us to pray that we will not succumb to temptation and, thus, be delivered into the web of evil. He wants us to pray that we will not get to that place in our life. Jesus wants us to resist so that Satan will flee from us (Jas 4:7). He wants us to put on the whole armor of God so that we can resist. He wants us to keep the faith so that he can use us, just as he wished for Peter (Lk 22:31.32).

Rewards

The rewards he wanted for Peter he also wants for us. We are promised a crown in heaven. A crown is an adornment for the head that signifies status. There are thirty different crowns mentioned in the Bible. Only a few are crowns of spiritual recognition that are promised as rewards to the redeemed souls in heaven. The crown given to us by the Lord will consist of multiple facets, each signifying an accomplishment, each recognizing our service on earth. These are crowns of rejoicing (1 Thes 2:19), crowns of righteousness (2 Thes 4:8), the crown of glory (1 Pt 5:4), and the crown of life (Jas 1:12), which is given to those who overcome Satan and the trials of life. It is given to those who keep their faith. It is the crown of an overcomer.

There are two kinds of tests we must overcome to get our crown of life.

Fleshly Tests

We must first overcome the fleshly tests: lust, greed, envy, covetousness, gluttony, jealousy, and anger. These open the door to demonic control. When we pray to be delivered from evil, we are asking God to protect us from the demonic powers trying to take control of our lives.

In the name of Jesus, we have authority to bind them and to rebuke their attempts to possess us. The fleshly temptations often are only irritating. In extreme situations, when the sin is not overcome, fleshly tests can lead to spiritual death—or even physical death when a disease such as AIDS is contracted as a result of the sin (Jas 1:15).

Rather than focus on the problem, I like to look at the solution. Remember this axiom: *Look where you are going, because you are going where you look.* If I spend all my time rebuking the power of darkness, my focus is turned from the solution to the problem. I prefer to spend my time praising my Lord who conquered our sin on his Cross, who once and for all overcame it, and who gave me a way to triumph over it. I praise him for his grace and for his power to overcome. When I give myself to the Holy Spirit, Satan's little helpers flee. I keep my eyes on him, not the problem.

Faith Tests

The more significant tests are the ones in which our faith, as well as our resolve, is tested. Tests of faith are painful tests; they involve our family, our wealth, our health, and our obedience to God. These tests take longer and are more difficult and challenging than the others. They test our integrity. Satan's goal is to get us to curse God and die (Jb 2:9).

I approach tests of faith in the same way as fleshly tests, but with a different intensity. The more difficult the test, the more I pray and praise. I know that the kingdom belongs to my Father, and the glory is his now and forever. When I wield the sword of the Spirit, Satan knows that is what I believe. When I prove that, by trusting God, the test usually abates, and I am a better man as a result. I know better that my God is one of deliverance. I have a deeper understanding of his love and a greater appreciation for the power of the Holy Spirit in my life.

One of those tests in my life caused so much doubt in my mind that I spent twenty years recovering from the experience. The first ten were so painful that I was on the verge of renouncing my faith and my salvation; I wanted my life to end. One night while praying, I laid my heart bare before the Lord and said that I could no longer go on in that condition.

That night, my wife was awakened by an angel standing by my side of the bed. She said that he stood for some time looking at me with a tear in his eye. She was unable to move until he said, "He will be okay."

When I awoke the next morning, I felt a sense of relief and had a new desire to see it through to the end. It took another ten years.

Recognizing Temptations

At times, I have failed the temptations of the flesh and the tests of faith, especially early in my Christian experience. Each time, I discovered God's grace, felt his mercy, and with my repentance came renewal in my heart. I don't like to be tested or tempted. I prefer to pray for protection from Satan. The best way for that to happen is to recognize what is in my heart and confess before God my sinful nature and ask him to remove it. God will put a hedge of thorns around the righteous, just as he did with Job.

Early in my Christian walk, I wasted a lot of energy trying to be perfect biblically. Every little sin threw me into a tailspin, and I worked that much harder to rid myself of it. In a short time, I became so frustrated that I allowed Satan to grab a significant foothold in my life. If nothing changes, why keep trying? I was trying to be perfect in my own strength. It didn't work so well.

Later in my life, after Satan lost his grip on me, I once again tried to be perfect in my own eyes. Every little sin was irritating me, and once more I began focusing on the problem instead of the solution. This time, instead of surrendering to Satan, I did something different.

One day while praying, I said, "Lord I don't like who I am, but I can't change me. The harder I try, the more I fail. I am tired of trying. You made me; it is up to you to change me. It is obvious I can't. If you don't make the changes, then you must like me the way I am." That was the moment I allowed Jesus to begin changing my heart. Instead of asking him to change my actions, I surrendered to him the source of my faults.

That may have been the second-best prayer I have ever prayed. At that moment, the Holy Spirit began his work in me. Like any sculpture, the big chunks came off quickly. In a short time, his man began to take shape. Since then the molding and remodeling have continued, and now my image is more like that of Christ.

The Work of God

I continually pray that God will not take me home until he has completed his work in me. It is my earnest prayer that when I meet my Lord in heaven, I will hear him say, "Look at what I did with Cole." I won't hear him say, "Well done, good and faithful servant," but I will wash his feet with my tears if I hear him say, "Look what I did with Cole!"

What do you want to hear him say?

Chapter 12
Facing the Demons

What do you believe? Life is dictated by what we think. Those who think a stove is hot when it is turned on will not touch it. People who know that electrical wires connected to a power source can inflict a shock won't touch them. People who believe they are ill will continue to seek medical help until they find a doctor who agrees with them. People who are convinced they must be able to see or touch something before it is real will have difficulty understanding or grasping the concept of a neutrino or even an atom. Both particles are too small for the eye to see, yet they are fundamental to the structure of our world.

Seen and Unseen

Some people believe there is nothing more to life than eating, drinking, and merriment because tomorrow you die and cease to exist. Religious people think that following rules, rituals, and giving allegiance to an idol created by their own imagination will make them acceptable to a god who is continually judging them.

Theirs is a lifeless god; one that has only the power they give to it. They create in their own mind the rules which they believe they can obey. As it was with Aaron, their image of God is nothing more than the golden calf they have created with their own hands; it is a lifeless, powerless idol they worship through rules and rituals (Ex 32:35).

People who are led by the Holy Spirit see things differently. They believe that things unseen affect the things seen. They understand that their actions are influenced by forces outside of their physical environment. Instead of worshiping as the Israelites did, a golden calf created from their imagination, they strive to worship a living entity by becoming sensitive to his will in their life.

I have known atheists and agnostics who sought guidance from mediums and fortune tellers. I know religionists who seek knowledge from the horoscope in the daily newspaper. I have also known Spirit-filled people who thought demons were behind every rock and crevice in their life. That caused them to spend so much time looking for the demons that they forgot to seek the Savior. What we believe impacts our behavior. Our experience affects our belief. My experience will continually triumph over another's theology and doctrine.

Profitable Doctrine

The Bible says that all scripture is given by inspiration of God and is profitable for doctrine, for reproof, for correction, for instruction in righteousness (2 Tm 3:16). When that instruction is applied correctly, the doctrine holds us fast to biblical truth. Problems arise when biblical interpretation is improperly used, then the resulting principle can become a millstone around our necks and a source of denial in the power of God, or it can lead to an abuse of his power. It becomes a vain philosophy of men.

Due to doctrine created by men who have interpreted God's Word in their own understanding, wooden idols have been built in the minds of many. Because a wooden god is worthless, many today are like children easily tossed too and fro by the doctrine of men and not the gospel of Christ (Jer 10:8; Eph 4:14). The gospel of Christ includes authority over demons (Mk 1:27; 3:14-15).

This chapter is not written as a manual on deliverance. Its purpose is to enlighten readers on the signs of demonic presence and convince them to seek help and guidance from those experienced in that area. It is also to set the reader free from the misunderstandings that have led many astray in their doctrine. My goal is to clarify the meaning and confusion that comes from improper use of the term *demon-possession*.

Do You Know?

Do you know of a Christian who continually struggles with sin in their life? Of course, you do. As I taught in the chapter on temptation, we all struggle with the sins of the flesh until, by testing and prayer, we overcome them. We live in two worlds. We live in the physical and the spiritual. What we want in the physical does not always agree with the spiritual (Rom 7:18; Gal 5:17). The Christian should aspire to bring the desires of the flesh into an agreement with the wishes of the Holy Spirit (Gal 5:16).

Are you aware of someone whose life revolves around pornography, someone who loves to indulge in pornographic images? Is that someone a Christian? Do they pray in repentance and fervently ask God to remove their longing? Yet their struggle goes on. Have you met someone who has gone to rehab multiple times, sought God's help, and still struggles with addiction? Have you ever felt a sudden stubborn resistance swell up within you that has kept you from doing something that you knew you should and may have even wanted to do? Where does that spirit of stubbornness come from?

Have you or someone you know had an irresistible urge to cause physical harm to another? Do you know someone who goes to bed angry and wakes up mad at the world? I wonder how many Christians like perverted sex and, even with prayer, can't let go of those desires. How many secretly lust over children? Does the need to look at pictures of naked children consume you?

You know that desiring your neighbor's property or their wife or husband is wrong, and you seek God's forgiveness, yet the desire never goes away. You make a good living, yet the drive for more consumes your life. Your family, your friends, your walk with God all comes in second to that desire. Do you go into a jealous rage anytime someone looks at your spouse? Are your thoughts, accusations, and intentions extreme? No matter how innocent the look, or their response to them, is your reaction out of control?

Are you someone who doesn't just like sex, you always crave it. You can't get enough. Is every person you are attracted to a potential conquest? Have you discovered they are willing? Does it seem as though you are irresistible, as though you are wearing love potion number 9? Have you found that opportunity is everywhere? No matter how much sex you get, you are never satisfied. Do you always want more, with different people, using various techniques, yet find it is never enough?

What about the bottle? Just can't put it down. You take one drink and can't quit until the bottle is empty. No matter how many times you have begged for God's forgiveness and promised your family that you will stop drinking, you don't. What about drugs? Rehab has dried you out, but the craving gnaws at you day and night. The voice in your head tells you that one little fix won't hurt.

Do you experience periods of heaviness, times when it feels like a cloud hangs over you, times when all energy leaves you and life doesn't seem worth living? Doctors call that depression; they treat it with medications designed to affect the chemical levels in the brain. If those drugs aren't working, perhaps there is another cause.

Do you know someone with multiple personalities? It could be they manifest them even to the point of using different names, or it could be someone just acting as though they were a different person at different times. The medical profession diagnoses this as Multiple Personality Disorder, but it has no known cause for this malady. The Bible does. It attributes this and many others to demonic possession.

Demonic Affliction

In the Bible, there is the story of a child with epilepsy who was cured when the demon was cast out (Mk 9:17-27). Demons also caused various sickness, blindness, paralysis, and extreme anger—which resulted in very aggressive behavior, and multiple personalities (Mt 4:24, 8:16, 8:33, 9:22, 12:22; Mk 5:15). There is an extensive list of sins attributed to unclean spirits (Mk 7:20-23; Lk 4:33). Demons cause migraines, back pain, and intestinal upsets in many.

If you have any of these problems or know someone who does, it may be that they are demonically afflicted. Wait a minute. You are a

Christian. You keep praying that God will take these desires from you, and yet you still struggle with them. You have an illness for which the doctors have no treatment and are uncertain of the cause.

Epilepsy has many causes, but idiopathic epilepsy is still one of the most commonly diagnosed forms of that condition. That diagnosis means the idiot (doctor) doesn't know why you have it. There are many idiopathic diseases; I wonder how many have demonic etiologies.

Maybe your pastor has told you that Christians can't be possessed by demons. He has said that they can't live in the presence of the Holy Spirit. How then could you be demon possessed? To answer that, let us look at this analogy. You own a boat that is stored at a friend's home. He can use it any time he wants. In that situation you own it; but who possesses it?

You made a confession of faith; you have been baptized for the repentance of your sin, and you have invited the Holy Spirit to take up residence in your life, but who was there before that happened? Do you think Satan and his demons are just going to throw up their hands in surrender and move out because the Holy Spirit wants to move in?

A Strong Man's House

Jesus said that no man can enter a strong man's house and plunder his goods unless he first binds the strong man (Mk 3:27). In other words, the demons you came to Christ with must be driven out before the Holy Spirit can take complete possession.

What about the statement Jesus made to Satan? You shall worship the Lord your God, and he only will you serve (Mt 4:10). Worship and service go hand in hand. We serve the one we worship, and in the end, we worship the one we serve. How does that happen?

Satan Dangles the Bait

King David is a perfect example of the effect of sin and worship, as the Bible teaches in 2 Samuel. In the spring of the year, when kings went to war, David decided to stay at home and delegate the fight to his generals. At that same time, Bathsheba bathed on the roof of her house. Every night, David watched her from his palace. That is why he stayed home. She was the hook that Satan baited for David. She knew David was looking and, as we say, she gave him his money's worth.

When David couldn't resist temptation any longer, he sent for her. He should have quit looking. She knew his intention when she was commanded to come to the palace. That is why she made a feeble protest by saying she was a married woman. David had taken the bait, and she was offering only weak resistance, just enough to set the hook.

At first, David practiced deceit and deception by bringing her husband, Uriah the Hittite, home from war. David hoped he could blame Bathsheba's expectant child upon him. When that didn't work, David arranged for his death in battle. His lust of the flesh led to theft, lies, deceit, and finally murder. He stole a man's wife and ultimately arranged that man's death.

These things did not lead to demon possession, but they did lead to a curse on his family. His child from this union died shortly after birth. His son Absalom took over his kingdom for a short while and caused a rebellion that led to his own death. David, when confronted by God, repented. Repentance is what kept Satan from possessing David (2 Sm 12, 13). But it did not prevent a curse from befalling him. The sins of the fathers shall follow our sons and daughters to the third or fourth generation (Nm 14:18; Ex 34:7).

Generational Curses

Most of my experiences with demons have been with people who were experiencing the curse placed upon them by their ancestors. Remember the Bible says the sins of the fathers shall be extended to the fourth generation. A curse is the consequence of disobedience to God. A curse of the Lord is on the house of the wicked, but he blesses the home of the just (Pr 3:33).

God, speaking to the priests of Israel through Malachi, said that if they did not hear his commandment and take it to heart, to give glory to his name, he would curse them and their blessings, that he would rebuke their descendants and take away the benefit of their worship (Mal 2:2-3). This sounds harsh, but I didn't make the rules; I just report what the Bible says.

Unclean Spirits

How then can a Christian be demon possessed? Jesus cast out what the Bible refers to as unclean spirits (Mk 7:29; Lk 4:33). These are spirits of evil thoughts, adultery, fornication, murder, theft, covetousness, deceit, lewdness, evil eye, blasphemy, pride, and foolishness (Mk 7:20-22). We can and do inherit these demons as a result of the sins of the parent. Instead of inheriting a blessing, some children inherit a curse because of the sins of their parents. The curse of the Lord is on the home of the wicked, but he blesses the home of the just (Pr 3:33).

From Generation to Generation

Curses result in poverty, sickness, and sin that reaches from generation to generation. The entire Bible is a story of sin and salvation. When people don't recognize the source of the sin, how will they discover the power of redemption? When Christians are taught that they can't be afflicted by a demonic presence, they are doomed to blame their bad luck, their aberrant behavior, and their overall misfortune on themselves or God's inability to save or to change them.

A doctor can't successfully treat a medical problem until the cause is identified. Christians can't be set free from demonic affliction until they realize they have a problem. Stink-n think-n keeps that from happening.

One way we acquire demons is through inheritance. The other way begins as it did with David. People look upon sin and discover its reward, and instead of repenting as David did, they continue in that sin. The longer they serve sin, the less they worship the Lord, and the more they worship Satan and follow his demons. He gives them the power to commit that sin continually.

In Service to One Master

After some time, they become a slave to the sin they commit. Christians may belong to God, but they are possessed by Satan. They become slaves of corruption; for by whom a person is overcome, he is also brought by him into bondage (2 Pt 2:19). Christ said no man can serve two masters. He said he will hate the one and love the other, or else he will be loyal to one and despise the other (Lk 16:13). These people place a curse upon themselves and their future offspring.

When I hear pastors say that Christians can't be possessed by demons, my heart cries out in sorrow for those who go through their life fighting with the same desires, not knowing there is an answer. As long as people don't realize they are under a curse, they are doomed to endure it. In that case, the doctrine they believe is harmful. When they don't understand the difference between possessing a demon and being demon possessed, they are easily led to disbelieve altogether and to think that God is unable to answer their prayers.

Who Dwells Within?

Christians must face two types of tests. The first is the test of the flesh. When we continually give in to the lusts of the flesh, we will ultimately become possessed by those demons. As we saw in David's case, adultery led to deceit, deception, and finally to murder. Jesus said that when a spirit goes out from a man, it finds a dry place, and then it says it will go back to the man. When he arrives, if he sees the house swept clean, he re-enters and invites his friends as well (Mt 12:43-45). When a house is cleaned, it is imperative that the person is filled with the Holy Spirit; otherwise the demons will return.

But this passage points out something else as well. It shows us that demons come in groups. Adultery goes with theft, lying, deceit, and even murder. Greed results in theft, deception, lying, and murder. Addictions have the same effect. Look at the lusts of the flesh. See how many go together! Greed and deceit are cut from the same cloth. Hate and anger can result in murder. Jealousy and slander keep each other company. Liars easily become thieves.

People who continually surrender to Satan, ultimately will be possessed by demons. Unless they repent and turn from their ways, their children will be plagued by the same sins to the fourth generation, and beyond, which actually translates to all succeeding generations, until one of those generations is set free through repentance and deliverance.

Keep the Faith

When Christians allow themselves to be controlled by the lusts of their heart, they will fail the test of their flesh, and are then vulnerable to tests of faith. Remember, Satan's purpose in that test is to cause one to lose their faith and to die in that condition. I once asked the Lord if it was possible to lose one's salvation. He asked me, "How were you saved?" I said, "By grace through faith." He replied, "Then don't lose it (faith)" (Eph 2:8; Col 1:19-23).

Satan's ultimate goal is to convince a Christian to renounce one's faith. Don't misunderstand me. Doubt is not the same as denouncing; we all doubt from time to time. There is no hope for the person who no longer believes in the Christ who died for them. There is no way to be saved except by the blood Jesus shed on the Cross (Heb 6:4-6). God will not turn loose of us; but we can, and some do, turn loose of him.

Satan tries our faith in many ways. The Holy Spirit and sin cannot live in harmony with each other, so a Christian's faith can be severely tested. The Bible teaches that a person cannot serve two masters. A person will love one and hate the other. The flesh lusts against the Spirit, and the Spirit lusts against the flesh, and these are contrary to one another (Gal 5:17).

Renounce Sins

If Christians don't renounce their sins, they will abandon their faith, unless God takes drastic steps. When Christians reach a point where the war within them is so intense that they can no longer stand the guilt they are feeling because of their sin, they must make a choice. If they make the wrong decision, Satan will own them.

The Bible says that for the person who is entangled in fleshly sins and overcome by them—a person brought again into bondage by the lusts of the flesh after they have escaped them through the knowledge of the Savior Jesus Christ—the end is worse than the beginning (2 Pt 2:18-20). These people become possessed by, controlled by, oppressed by demons. Their life becomes a living hell because of the war going on within them.

This happens when Christians continually quench the Holy Spirit by committing acts of unrepentant sin. Then at some point in time, they decide to serve Satan instead of God; at that point, Satan possesses them. They are under his control.

Christians must understand that demons are real. Biblical references to them are not metaphors for sin in general or examples of Christ catering to first-century superstition. The Bible is a story of spiritual truth. God is a spirit and must be worshiped as such (Jn 4:24). We live in a world controlled by an evil spirit. When we come to that realization, we will be able to see sin for what it is. Sin is the result of *the acts of demonic spirits combined with the nature of our flesh to combat the will of a living God.*

Deliverance From Curses

In our enlightened—but blind—society, we say addictions are genetic. The scripture declares them family curses. They may have a genetic basis in some cases, such as alcoholism, but they stem from the evil our ancestors did, and those curses must be broken for a cure to occur.

That can only be done through repentance and deliverance. Sex addiction is not inherited; it is demon possession. Greed is a form of gluttony that requires repentance and deliverance. The curse of jealousy can only be cured by repentance and deliverance. Any family trait that is not from God is in all likelihood a curse that needs breaking.

If you are a Christian who continually fights the same sinful desire, and you have prayed earnestly for forgiveness and for God to take it away to no avail, you may have a demon problem. I have been involved in a deliverance ministry, and the only people who could be delivered through that work were Christians. They were the only ones we had a legal right to set free. The others belonged to Satan, and unless they renounced his work in their life and invited Jesus into their heart, our group had neither the authority nor the power to deliver them. If you need deliverance, seek out those who are gifted in this way.

Owning the Demonic

Demon possession has two meanings; they both refer to ownership. In the first case, the person owns the demon. It came to them either by family curse or by invitation. Many people court the demonic. I knew people in Oregon who attended psychic fairs. While there, they had their fortunes told, bought statues devoted to idols, consulted mediums, and in other ways invited the demonic into their lives.

Some people acquire their demons through their lust. When Satan recognizes an opportunity, he takes it. He will send one to empower the lustful and enable them to engage in that activity continually. The more they participate, the more control the demon has over them. When the measure of their sin is full (1 Thes 2:16), the demons have them. The Holy Spirit is no longer in control. The devil enables them to fulfill the lust of their heart.

Demon Owned

The second way that the term demonic possession is used means to be owned by the demons. In the first situation, the person owns the demon and can with difficulty resist them. In the second, the devils own the person. This happens when the individual completely surrenders to them. These people become schizophrenics, paranoiacs, and people with multiple personalities. Possessed people may be serial killers, serial rapists, and child molesters. Their addictions are uncontrollable and incurable unless they are delivered. Whatever their proclivity, it will be excessive and severe.

Holy Spirit Doctrine

Can a Christian be demon possessed? First, let me restate a fact: They can have demons either from inheritance or invitation before becoming a Christian. Can they become possessed by the demons after becoming a Christian? At this point doctrine and theology get in the way of our understanding. Many teachers say that Christians can't be possessed by demons because of the Holy Spirit living in them. Some teach that all Christians are filled with the Holy Spirit when they are baptized in the name of Jesus for the remission of sins (Acts 2:38), and others believe that the Baptism in the Spirit can be a separate event (Acts 8:15,16).

When Christians of either persuasion refer to being filled with the Holy Spirit, in their minds they are thinking of the baptism of, with, or in, the Holy Spirit, as represented in various scriptures in the book of Acts and when Jesus was baptized by John. The preposition used to denote that baptism is of minimal importance. The concept is the message.

As it was with Jesus, the baptism of the Holy Spirit is when he comes upon us to empower us to do the works of Jesus and to light our fire. If you have no power, if your fire (enthusiasm) has never burned, you have not been baptized by the Holy Spirit (Mt 3:11; Acts 1:8).

The Holy Spirit lives in us, with us, and comes upon us. He walks with us to teach and to guide us. He makes us one with Jesus and with the Father. He gives us the authority that Christ had and the anointing that we need to do the work God intends for us. All of that comes when we are baptized in the Spirit.

Being Spirit-filled is not the same as being baptized in the Spirit. What does being Spirit-filled mean? The best way I can describe that is to use three identical glasses as an example. The first 12-ounce glass is filled to the brim with water and nothing else; the second glass has a few cubes of ice placed in it before filling it with water; and the third glass is filled first with ice and then water. All three glasses are said to be filled with water, but each of them holds a different amount because of the ice.

That same analogy can be applied to Christians and the Holy Spirit. When the Holy Spirit comes into our heart, he must reside with the old man and the demons that came with him. As the old man is gradually replaced by the new man, more room is made for the Holy Spirit, and the new man can hold more of him.

Christ differed from us in the amount of the Holy Spirit he received. The old King James Bible says that Jesus, the one whom God has sent, to him he has given the Holy Spirit without limit (Jn 3:34). Be careful with the Bible translation you read. One has changed the wording so that the meaning is altered to say the Holy Spirit is given to everyone without limit.

That may be why some teach that we receive all of the Holy Spirit we will ever have when we accept Jesus. Contextual reading of that verse does not support the broader interpretation and, in my experience, this is just not true.

When I was baptized by the Holy Spirit, I received power, and a fire was lit within me. The way I have walked with him has determined the amount of energy and the brightness of that fire.

Scripture says how much more your Father, who is in heaven, will give good things to those who ask him (Mt 7:11). What is better than the Holy Spirit in a Christian's life? Jesus said first seek the kingdom of God, and then all other things will be given to you. The kingdom only comes by the Holy Spirit.

The Parable of the Talents

Christ taught the parable of the talents. This is a story about using the gifts of the Spirit which we have been given (Mt 25:14-29). It points out that some are given more gifts of the Spirit than others; but the more we use our gifts, the more he will provide us with. The closer we walk with the Holy Spirit, the fuller we become. Being filled with the Holy Spirit is a daily process; being baptized by the Holy Spirit is a one-time event.

In any case, if you want more Holy Spirit, create a bigger container. If you want the demons to have less influence, make sure that cup is continually filled with the Holy Spirit. Can a Christian, after being baptized in the Holy Spirit, become possessed by demons? I doubt it as long as the person's cup is not *empty*, but one can be oppressed by demons. Every Christian is tempted and tested by Satan's devils.

More Than Conquerers

Christians who have been baptized in the Holy Spirit and who wear the whole armor of God daily have all the protection they need to deflect the darts of the devil and to resist his demons. Christ through the Holy Spirit has given us authority over all power of Satan and his henchmen (Lk 9:1, 10:19; Jn 17:20).

Satan can test our faith. God allows that to purify the faith that is in us. Sometimes the tests of faith can be quite intense. As long as a Christian does not lose their faith, Satan cannot have them. I do know how close I have come to that state and what the Lord did to deliver me. I appreciate what Peter meant when he said how much worse off that person would be if they again became entangled in the sins of their heart after they had been set free by our Lord.

Identify the Adversary

I know there is a lot to digest in this chapter. If you are going to pray to win, it is essential to understand what you are up against and to understand how to find the answers. People can't be freed from demons that they don't know they have. Curses cannot be broken until they are recognized.

We war not against flesh and blood but against powers and principalities, rulers of darkness, and spiritual hosts of wickedness in heavenly places (Eph 6:12). Those who allow them to win the war in the heavens are doomed to fight them in their own flesh.

Chapter 13
Thine Is

Jesus concludes the model prayer with the statement, "Thine is the kingdom, the power, and glory forever. Amen." It is important to remember the principles of the kingdom as we conclude our prayer. The first principle is ownership. It is his kingdom. We are his subjects. He is Lord; we are not. That is why it is equally important to end our prayer as we begin it. We should leave his court with praise for the way he will answer our prayer, and we should exit his gates with thanksgiving for the privilege of coming before him, while giving thanks to him for the answers he gives to our prayers.

The psalmist gave thanks to the Lord, and says, "I will praise him for he is my God, and I will exalt him. Give thanks to the Lord for he is good: for his mercy endures forever" (Ps 118:28, 29). "The angel of the Lord encamps around those who fear God, and he delivers them. O taste and see that the Lord is good: blessed is the man that trusts in him" (Ps 34:7, 8).

Without faith, it is impossible to please God. We must believe that he is and that he rewards those who diligently seek him (Heb 11:6). Jesus encountered a fig tree one day, and being hungry he went to it looking for fruit. When he discovered there was none, he pronounced a curse upon the tree, and immediately it began to wither (Mt 21:18, 19).

When the disciples asked how it was possible the tree withered away so soon, Jesus answered and said that if they had faith and did not doubt, they could not only do this to the fig tree, but if they said to this mountain, "be removed and be cast into the sea," it would be done. Whatever you ask in prayer, believe, and it shall be done (Mt 21:20-22).

Jesus wasn't speaking of a literal mountain but was referring to the mountain of disbelief. He was talking about the curse of non-productivity. The fig tree should have been producing fruit. It was in season. It had leafed out and should have been producing. Like many Christians, it wasn't. We allow the mountains of disbelief to overcome our production.

Satan has tried, with each chapter of this book, to convince me that no one will read it. He has told me no one wants to know what I have learned over fifty-plus years of walking with God. With each chapter, I have prayed, "God give me your words, your thoughts, show me how," and I have continued to type. Prayer is like that. We must continue to pray, but in that, we must believe that God is who he says he is and does what he says he will, and we must think he will do it for us.

Faith is not telling God what to do and then holding out until he does it. It trusts him to do what he wants, when he wants, and the way he wants. It humbles us to his will and his plan. It believes in the authority of the Word of God and in its promises.

On many occasions, I have heard people pray a perfectly good prayer and at the conclusion negate all they have said by their lack of faith. They say things like, "Nevertheless, God, if it is your will," or make some other negative statement that demonstrates a lack of faith.

As you read the Psalms, many of which are prayers, notice that they end with a positive repetition of the way they began. If you believe that God hears and answers prayer, then conclude that prayer with thanksgiving for the answer, for the way it will come and the one who makes it possible. Praise him for his power to make it happen and be grateful to him for your relationship with the Holy Spirit and the strength he puts into you.

Charles Stanley has said, *Power in God's kingdom is his divine energy placed in us to complete his divine purpose through us.* That power comes as a result of our faith in him and in the Holy Spirit working through us. Failure to believe and to obey keeps us from being available to the Spirit.

One Sunday as I left the church, I heard myself mutter to God, "Just think what we could do if all the power of the Holy Spirit were available to me." In one step, I heard him say, "Just think what we could do if you were available to all the power of the Holy Spirit." My lack of faith and the resulting disobedience keeps that from happening. Paul said that we each have gifts as a result of God's grace and that we should use them according to the faith in us (Rom 12:6). At times in my life, there has been very little faith and even less production. A king will not let the people of his kingdom down if he knows they trust in him, especially when they are working for him.

> *Just think what we could do if you were available to all the power of the Holy Spirit.*

Homecoming

A woman of faith shared this story with me. The year was 1953. Sarah and Bill had been married only two months when he was drafted. The Korean War was going on, and the men knew that was where they would be sent. Sarah went to live with Bill's parents. Every night she went to the Lord and pleaded with him to get Bill discharged from the army. On one occasion, she shared her request with her sister and said that she knew the Lord was going to answer her prayer.

Her sister chastised her. She told her never to tell anyone else what she was praying. She said God couldn't answer such a prayer. The only way Bill could get out of the army was to be dishonorably discharged or severely injured.

Have you ever burst into a flame of faith and had someone who was well-meaning douse it with a bucket of realism? That is what happened to Sarah. After her sister's comments, she went to the Lord and said, "Lord, please forget what I have been asking you to do. I don't want something terrible to happen to my husband."

Just as she arose from her knees, the Holy Spirit spoke to her and said, "Don't you know that God has all power? He has more power than the United States Army." She returned to her knees and made a positive confession of faith. "I know you can bring him home, God. I know that he doesn't have to be sick or injured. I don't know how, but I know you can and will."

One day she shared with her sister that Bill was coming home, that God was going to answer her prayer. Her sister said that she never wanted to hear her say that again. God couldn't do that, and she needed to have her head tested. Sarah resolved to never speak of it to her sister again but to continue to believe God would answer her prayer.

In a short time, she received a letter from her husband saying he was coming home. His boot had rubbed a sore on his foot, causing an infection that sent him to the hospital for a month. Because of that, he had not finished his basic training. Just as he was about to start his training again, an army doctor reviewed his medical record and recommended that he be discharged.

If he got another infection, it would result in the loss of his foot. God brought him home, healthy and without a dishonorable discharge. The foot never gave him another problem. That act of faith on Sarah's part and God's answer caused her sister to accept Jesus as her Lord. It brought glory to God.

Obedience

There is a component of faith that goes beyond belief: obeying God. We believe that God can; we trust that he will. But there is an overlooked component to trust that we must address. It is obedience. Why do we disobey God? Is it is because we don't really believe? Is it because we put our desires over his? Do we believe but fail to trust? How many times have you refused when God has asked something of you? Was it because you didn't think he could or would deliver? Why didn't you trust him? If you believed him, why didn't you obey him?

On Thursdays, I ride with a group of motorcyclists. On this day, I was asked to pray for the groups' protection and God's blessing. As I usually do, I thanked God for the protection he would give us, and for the angel he would send to clear our path and watch over us.

Acting as the leader of the pack, I chose the road on which we returned home. As we approached a particular intersection, I felt an urging to continue on through to the next light and take that street. Instead, I decided to ignore the voice in my head and turn onto our usual route. Circumstances caused the man behind me to fail to notice that I was turning, and he crashed into the back of my bike.

God's spirit was doing his part; I wasn't listening to him. For two blocks I had heard his voice encouraging me to go straight, and yet I ignored him. Why? I didn't intentionally disobey him. It wasn't that I didn't trust him. I didn't realize he was the one talking to me.

Since then I have intensified my prayer request to become so sensitive to the Holy Spirit that I will know even his most subtle whisper, feel whatever he is feeling, and never again ignore his voice. When I hear the soft whisper that is his, I intend to believe it is him, instead of me, and to respond in faith and obedience to his command.

If we are going to confess that it is his kingdom, his power, and his glory, we must be able to recognize his commands, know his will, and obey. I am determined to respond to that slight whisper that is the Holy Spirit. I have willfully disobeyed God and paid a heavy price for that. I have unintentionally disobeyed and suffered the consequences of that. My sincere prayer is that I will become so sensitive to the Holy Spirit that I will never be guilty of either again.

Obedience Can Bring Protection

I want to be more like Sarah. She shared with me another story of her prayer life. One day while she was praying, the Holy Spirit spoke and told her to go and lock her storm door. At first, she ignored him and continued to pray. Again she heard him, and yet she ignored his warning. The third time he spoke to her, she ceased her prayer and went to the door. Just as she locked it, a car stopped in her driveway and a man got out.

He said that he was interested in buying her house and wondered if he could come in. Sarah told him that her home wasn't for sale and he couldn't enter. At that, he grabbed the door and tried to force it open. The lock held, and Sarah was able to close and lock the main entrance. She hollered that she was calling the police, and the man left.

The next day her son's friend told him that a man came to his house and tricked his mother into letting him in. The stranger attacked her, and just as he was forcing himself upon her, the phone rang, and she was able to knock the receiver from the cradle and scream for help. At that, the man left; in a short time, the police arrived. From the description, it was the same man who came to Sarah's.

Obedience isn't just in the big things; it is in the smallest, as well. Without faith, it is impossible to please God (Heb 11:6). It is his kingdom. It is his power. It is his glory, and it will all be his forever and forever. To participate in that kingdom, we must believe, trust, and above all else, obey. Doing that allows us to bring glory to him.

Inheriting the Kingdom

Our God can meet all our needs according to his glorious riches in Jesus Christ (Phil 4:19). Of course, there is a contingency that must be remembered: the wicked cannot expect to benefit from the kingdom. The Bible says do not be deceived, the unrighteous will not inherit the kingdom of God.

Because of their sin, the unrighteous cannot live in the kingdom of God. That list includes those committing sexual sins, idolaters, thieves, the covetous, drunkards, revilers, and extortioners. Many of these are sins that we excuse today, but Paul says they have no place in God's kingdom. (1 Cor 6:9-10).

The Lord is a sun and a shield; he bestows favor and honor; no good thing does he withhold from those whose walk is blameless (Ps 84:11). *Intentional sinners* do not live in the kingdom of God on earth, and they will not inherit the one to come.

To live in his kingdom and to bring honor to him, it is essential to understand the law of giving. Give and it will be given unto you. A good measure, pressed down, shaken together and running over, will be poured out unto you. For with the measure you use, it will be measured unto you (Lk 6:38).

What We Bind on Earth

If we are going to use God's power, we must believe that whatever we bind on earth will be bound in heaven, and whatever we loose on earth will be loosed in heaven (Mt 16:19). It is necessary to place his will above our need. Jesus said that we should seek first the kingdom of God and his righteousness and all other things would be given to us. Therefore, there is no need to worry about tomorrow (Mt 6:33-34).

Through our prayers and giving the Holy Spirit the freedom to do his work, we are brought into the kingdom of God, and by living in that kingdom we are given the blessings we long for. The psalmist said to delight thyself in the Lord and he would give you the desires of your heart (Ps 37:4) When we desire him to be first in our life, all other desires will be given to us. When we bind the evil in our heart which opposes that and release the desire for God to be first in our life, God will hear from heaven and instruct the Holy Spirit to make it happen. This means he will give us the desires we should have. It doesn't mean he will fulfill for us the desires of the flesh that we do have, although he will give us the blessings we need.

Freely Give

It is equally important to understand that this law of the kingdom also contains another truth: Jesus said that we should heal the sick, cleanse the lepers, raise the dead, and cast out demons. He said, "Freely you have received, now freely give" (Mt 10:8). Everything in God's kingdom is free. We can pay for nothing, but we do owe for everything. Having been set free from sin, we have become slaves to righteousness (Rom 6:18). The thing that keeps many from doing that is the failure to understand the necessity to receive and how it must be done.

Many do not feel forgiven because they think they must earn it. These people do not receive it as a free gift. Some who are lost cannot be saved because they do not receive salvation freely. They cannot believe that their only role in the process is to accept this gift of grace. They cannot pay for it (Rom 3:23-26). Everything in God's kingdom is free, and it must be received that way so that it can be given in the same manner. Those who do not understand this principle will never be able to walk in the power of God. They are like Simon, who tried to buy the ability to lay hands on people so that they might receive the Holy Spirit. He wanted to buy and then sell a free gift from God (Acts 8:18-21).

Those who do not learn to receive freely and believe they must earn God's gifts, which are a product of his grace, are doomed like Simon to perish, because their heart is not right in the sight of God. Unless they repent and learn to accept what God has for them willingly, they will receive nothing but condemnation.

What those who walk in his power must also understand is that it is his glory they seek. To him belong the kingdom, the power, and the glory. God's gifts are not for our recognition but are to exalt Jesus. The Bible says that those who have received a gift should minister it to others as they received it (freely).

A Joyful Noise

Those who speak should speak the Words of God. Those who minister should do so with all the power God has given them so that in all things God would be glorified in Jesus Christ to whom belongs the glory and dominion forever and ever (1 Pt 4:10-11). Living in God's kingdom is not about our recognition. It is about his. When we bring glory to him, he will give glory to us (Jn 17:22).

Because it is his kingdom, his power, and his glory forever, God deserves to be worshiped. I have heard many who claim to be Christians say that they only go to church to listen to a good sermon, not to do all that singing. It is my opinion that the person who does not want to do all that singing and does not want to worship God, does not walk in his kingdom here, and probably will not in heaven.

There will be no sermons in heaven, only praise and worship. Those who won't worship him here will not fit in there. If you just don't like to sing, double up on your adoration in your prayer time. If you are like me and can't carry a tune, make a joyful noise as you praise and worship him in prayer.

Worship and serve the Lord your God, and his blessing will be on your food and water. He will take away sickness from you, and none will be barren or miscarry in your land. He will give you a full lifespan (Ex 23:25-26). His angel will go before you and be an adversary to your adversaries (Ex 23:20-22). Remember, we serve the one we worship (Mt 4:10). Understand that the God of the Bible is a jealous God (Ex 34:14), so do not provoke him to wrath by serving another.

So I Believe

Jesus concludes the model prayer with the word *Amen*. This word says only one thing: *It is so*. Amen comes at the end of the prayer, but its definition does not mean the prayer is over. It is a statement of truth and belief. I believe, thus it is so. Because it is, so I believe. Faith is belief. It knows that God's Word and his promises are real. When we say amen, it had better be a statement that the issue is settled. Then wearing the helmet of salvation and carrying the shield of faith will protect us from the fiery darts of doubt, and faith will motivate God to act on our behalf.

Chapter 14
Healing the Wounds

This chapter is for Christians and church members who have been wounded. It is a chapter God wants to be written, and one that should be read. I have been a church member over fifty years; I have served as a teacher, deacon, and elder; and I filled the role of assistant pastor. The things I say in this chapter come from that experience.

Why am I opening this chapter by referring to the church? Isn't it about healing wounds? It is a chapter about healing all of them. There are two kinds of injuries. Both need healing: Some scars are caused by other people, and some are self-inflicted. In this chapter, I want to show how they can both be healed.

Self-Inflicted Wounds

Let us look first at the self-inflicted wounds. Most of these wounds are deliberate. They result from self-destructive habits or desires. Some people fulfill a need by cutting themselves, others by starving themselves. Some find solace in the bottle or the needle.

Soon, many in this country will smoke marijuana habitually, now that we have endorsed medical marijuana and are using that as an excuse for drug legalization. When many have no short-term memory and are incapable of holding jobs or getting through their day without a puff, we will understand that the nation has made a legal way for many to suffer self-inflicted wounds. Children raised in homes with parents smoking this drug will bear wounds inflicted by others, the same as those using the product. Second-hand inhalation of the smoke is just as toxic as actually smoking the product.

Many of us have wounds inflicted by parents with poor child-rearing techniques. I know of no job more difficult than child rearing. Unfortunately, most of us raise our children by emulating the methods our parents used, or by saying "not ever" and then doing just the opposite. Parents, with the best of intentions, can wound their children. Most of the time, they are unaware of the wounds they inflict. Very few parents deliberately want to harm their children.

Physical wounds heal with time and, hopefully, teach us to be more careful, more aware of our surroundings. If we are lucky, these wounds leave us with no lasting problems. Those who aren't fortunate may end up crippled in some manner. Spiritual injuries are different. These are the mental wounds that affect our inner person. They cripple us for life, unless healed. The hurt does not go away until inner healing occurs. It is easy to take these injuries, box them up, and lock them away in the deepest corner of our heart.

By refusing to look at them, we go through life needing to protect ourselves from them, determined never to let that happen again. Some people practice avoidance as the best way to do that: don't take a risk and then failure won't occur. Some feel the need to be in control and by doing that think they can protect themselves from hurt. Our fears keep us from being all that we can be. They cause us to react in ways that negatively impact our lives and the lives of others.

The Reluctant Receiver

For all of us, inner healing begins with love. The love of a caring spouse or other caring individuals may help start the process. Complete healing requires the individual to discover the true healer and to allow him to do his work. Many years ago, I was invited by my office manager, Betty, to attend a Holy Spirit conference. I didn't want to go, but because Betty had spent so much time praying for me and because I valued her walk with the Lord, I agreed.

The first night, the speaker explained the gifts of the Spirit and demonstrated how they worked, especially the Word of knowledge. At the conclusion of the service, he announced that five men in the audience had back problems and said that he wanted each of them to come to the front of the room and ask two men to pray for their healing. He said God would do that for them.

Four went up, and I sat in my chair, saying to myself, "No way." After some time, the speaker said we are waiting for the fifth man; we will not begin until he comes here. I was amazed at his confidence in what he had heard from the Lord and was starting to wonder if I might miss out on a blessing. With reluctance and timidity, I walked forward.

A young man in his late teens or early twenties came and asked if he could pray for me. He wondered if anyone else would join us. I said no. He would do. He began to pray, and nothing happened. I was not receiving the prayer. That is why Jesus asked some, who were in need of healing, what they wanted (Lk 18:41): "What do you want?"

In my case, pride and doubt stood in my way. Some people just don't want what Jesus has to offer and others, like me, may want it but aren't willing to receive because of pride or for other reasons. In every instance, his gifts must be accepted as they are offered, freely.

The young man asked why I had back problems, and I explained that I had broken my knee in a motorcycle accident while in college. I said that knee would not straighten completely, causing an unhealthy tilt to my pelvis and lower back. Once more, the young man began to pray. Seeing the fragility of his faith, I was willing to receive, not for my sake, but for his. Not for my hope, because I had none, but for his.

I whispered, "Lord, I don't expect you to heal me, but I would like to see you do something for this young man's sake. I don't want to see him disappointed." At that moment, it felt like this man had placed his hand on my right knee, the one that I had broken but had not identified, and upon my lower back.

I said to myself, *he can't touch me like that, especially in public.* When I opened my eyes, I saw him standing three feet from me with his eyes closed. Then I knew those were the hands of Jesus. All of a sudden, I felt the bones in my back go *snap, snap*, and I received the healing power of God. It has been over forty years, and I have never had a problem with my back since then.

That night I received physical healing; the next day I received inner healing. The first night of this two-part conference, I didn't want to go, but I did. The next day, even after receiving his healing, I really didn't want to be there. I discovered how much pressure Satan can bring to bear when he wants to deprive us of God's blessing. After wrestling with my own resistance, I reluctantly arrived. The talk that day was a continuation of the explanations of the gifts of the Holy Spirit. By the end of it, I had relaxed and let down my guard.

The speaker said that we should allow ourselves to have others pray for us. They should pray as the Holy Spirit led. My office manager asked if she could pray for me. Of course, I said yes. That permission did not include the four women sitting around me. The moment Betty began to pray, the others jumped in. As much as I wanted, I was unable to resist the touch of these women.

Soon, I heard one of them come against my fears. I laughed to myself. I wasn't afraid of anything. At least nothing I was going to admit. Just then one of the others began to call out some of them. They were fears locked deep in the closet of my heart, and I started to melt under the power of the Spirit.

One at a time, each of my hidden fears was called out and healed by the power of the Holy Spirit. The process took most of an hour, and by then, I was Jello in the hand of the Lord. My experience left me weak and unable to move. When he completed the healing process, the Holy Spirit had them pray for my strength and faith in the coming days.

At the time, I had no idea why I would need that strength and faith. I soon found out. Two days later I received a phone call from my pastor, a man with whom I had worked closely for ten years, and I heard him invite me to an elders meeting that night. At that meeting, he branded me as a "charismatic." He used my attendance at this conference on the Holy Spirit as proof and demanded that I leave his church.

He said we were Baptist and didn't believe in that stuff; he would not tolerate it. He thought that all the gifts and acts of the Holy Spirit ceased when the last Apostle died. He said that, now, God only works through closed doors in a person's life.

I was forbidden to mention the Holy Spirit again in his church. If I couldn't agree to that, I would have to leave. Instead of offering a defense, all I said was that I couldn't choose which parts of the Bible I wanted to believe. I had to either accept it all or none, and I wished them well as I walked away.

That was a painful, gut-wrenching time in my life. It was a time of mourning for me. That church was my family. I was tempted to anger. But because of the prayers of those ladies, all I felt was sorrow for the pastor. How could any man serving God be so blind? Once that label was placed upon me, a few of my friends in the church refused to speak to me. They made it clear they didn't believe as I did.

That didn't surprise me. I understood that the members of a church think as the pastor has taught them. Just as the workers in a company take on the attitude of the boss, church members believe the doctrine taught by the pastor-—right or wrong.

I thank God for the work the Holy Spirit did in me before that day. Had I not been cleansed of those fears and wounds inflicted by my childhood, I probably would have been so disillusioned that I might have turned my back on God, and definitely would have done so with the church forever. Anger would have prevailed instead of sorrow.

The experiences of our lives inflict a lot of wounds. Most of them are spiritual in nature; some are physical as well. Those who have experienced physical injuries can be crippled because of bitterness. Some people, in spite of their wounds, make the best of a bad thing. How that wound is handled spiritually will determine who these people become.

Witnessing God's Goodness

I have a good friend, Larry, in Oregon who has every right to be bitter. At the beginning of his productive life, just as he approached thirty, he received the diagnosis of Multiple Sclerosis (MS). In a short time, he had to give up his job. I never once heard him complain. He only said, "God is good." As his physical abilities began to decline, he witnessed all the more of God's goodness.

In a few years, his wife was diagnosed with breast cancer. By then, she was the breadwinner for the family. While undergoing surgery and chemo, she continued to teach. I don't know how she found the strength to stand before her class during that process. While this was going on, one of Larry's brothers died of colon cancer, and all I heard Larry say was, "God is good." In a few more years Larry's wife had her second breast removed. All I heard him say was, "God is good."

Larry had one other brother, Skip. When Skip was diagnosed with MS, Larry understood what Skip would be facing, and yet all I heard him say was, "God is good."

Each time Larry was admitted to the hospital, it became an opportunity for him to witness of God's goodness. In the midst of his pain and discomfort, I never heard Larry say anything other than that God is good. Skip went downhill much faster than Larry, and in a short time Skip was admitted to a nursing home. Skip also used his affliction as an opportunity to testify of the goodness of God. I know that Larry's encouragement made that possible.

When Skip died, Larry said, "God is so good." When I watch a man spend all those years enduring declining health, having no hope of recovery, and yet never hear him say anything but God is good, I am ashamed of my frailty and lack of faith and am buoyed by his. When I see how God has taken everything the devil has thrown at this family and made from it something good, all I can say is, "God is so good."

Although I don't want to trade places with Larry, I envy the opportunities he has had to lead others to Christ through his affliction. I am in awe of his ability to praise God in the midst of constant suffering. Without a lot of prayers and the love of God, all of that faith could just as quickly have become bitterness.

Then instead of a life of joy and peace through the Holy Spirit, it would have been one of hate-filled anger. Because God is so good, Larry has raised children who know Jesus as Lord, and who are leading others to Christ. His wife was healed of cancer, twice; and through it all, they have been sustained by the love of Christ, which is all the fullness of God. Through suffering, they have brought glory to God.

The Commission

When Jesus left the wilderness, and after he had overcome the devil's temptations, the Bible says that he went to the synagogue in Nazareth. There, he opened the book of Isaiah and read what was written: it was the commission he was given by the Holy Spirit. He was anointed to preach the gospel to the poor. He was sent to heal the brokenhearted, to proclaim liberty to the captives and recovery of sight to the blind. He came to set at liberty those who are bruised (oppressed) and to announce the acceptable year of the Lord (Lk 4:18-19).

This commission was one of healing and hope. The people of Nazareth rejected him and what he offered. They were not willing to *receive*. I have discovered the most significant impediment to God's blessings is our failure to accept them. Some, like me, want first to earn his gifts; others don't think of themselves as worthy; and pride keeps some from receiving his blessings. Church leaders frequently fall into the latter category. Instead of preparing the membership to do the work of the church, some leaders think they should be doing the job. All the attention should be on the leaders.

It is essential to understand the commission given to Jesus. He says that he came to heal the brokenhearted, restore sight to the blind, to proclaim liberty to the captives, and to set the oppressed (bruised) free. The Bible says that God anointed Jesus of Nazareth with the Holy Spirit and power (the two always go together), and he went about doing good and healing all who were oppressed by the devil (Acts 10:38).

Bondage

In the forty-four instances in which the word *oppressed* is used in scripture, it is a reference to Satan or his representatives oppressing someone (having power over them). In the eighty-eight times the word *captive* is used, it is a reference to people taking someone or something captive. So who were the captives that Jesus referred to? How did he intend to liberate them, and from what?

Satan oppresses people and some he takes captive. His demons have power only to work through people. By themselves, they can accomplish nothing. They must attach themselves to the sins of a person's heart and then work by motivating that person to carry out their will. When demons exert their power over that person, the person is oppressed; in many cases, that oppression leads to sickness.

The Bible says Jesus went about healing all who were oppressed by the devil (Acts 10:38). When prayed for, these physical healings, which have spiritual causes, are frequently instantaneous; but in some cases, healing can be most difficult. In certain situations, the authority given to the demons must be revoked by the oppressed person before healing can occur.

In the scripture, people are made captive by the actions of others. In all eighty-eight scriptural references, people took others captive; but in many instances, spiritual iniquity made it possible. Who did Jesus minister unto? He said that he was sent only to the lost sheep of the house of Israel (Mt 15:24).

Jesus came to set the people of the house of Israel free from the captivity of religion, not that imposed by the Romans. He wanted to open their blind eyes to the truth. In the beginning, God gave them ten simple commandments, which would enable them to live righteously with him and to have peace with each other. Instead of teaching people to take those commandments into their hearts, the rulers of the synagogue and the religious leaders took those commandments and turned them into six hundred and thirty rules, many designed to make an exception to the laws of God.

In doing that, they were able to enslave the house of Israel and to take captive its members. Jesus, with his teaching, came to set them free from the rules of man and to show them how to write those laws of God into their heart. Jesus doesn't want people to be religious: he wants them to be spiritual.

Because the house of Israel did not receive him and his teaching, they must now be brought to that realization by going through "Jacob's Trouble," as the Old Testament calls it, or the "Tribulation," as it is called in the New Testament. God says this is the Covenant I will make with the house of Israel. After those days (that is the time of Jacob's Trouble or the Tribulation), I will put my laws in their mind and write them upon their heart, and I will be their God, and they shall be my people (Heb 8:10). Those laws can only be written into our hearts by the Holy Spirit.

Jesus came to set the Jews free from religion. All religion is a form of bondage. Men and their doctrine teach people rules of behavior but do nothing to write them into the heart. Religion convicts people of guilt and binds them to their sin, thus enslaving them to the institution it has created. By following the rules of the institution, they have a hope of salvation, but because the institution continually reminds them of their sinful nature, they are never taught to be free of their sin.

Set Free

Jesus said that if the son makes you free, you will be free indeed (Jn 8:36). Paul taught that through one man's offense, judgment came to all men, but that through one man's righteous act, the free gift of grace came to all men (Rom 5:18-19). The problem is that men seem to want to be under the law instead of being set free by the blood of Jesus. Instead of living by the power of the Holy Spirit, they place themselves under the law and become captives to religion once again.

Pastors enable that captivity by teaching Sunday after Sunday that their people are sinners; they continue to emphasize the sins instead of showing them how to be the saints the Bible says we become upon salvation. Those who are baptized into Christ Jesus are baptized into his death. If that is so, then just as he was raised from the dead to the glory of the Father, we should walk in the newness of life (Rom 6:3-4). He who has died with Christ has been freed from sin (Rom 6:7). Therefore, do not place yourselves again under the law. Sin shall not have dominion over you; you are under grace unless you put yourself under the law (Rom 6:13-14). Preachers and teachers need to encourage a life set free in the Holy Spirit, instead of one constrained by bondage.

Jesus came to set us captives free by writing the laws of God into our hearts, and those who live by the Holy Spirit have the power to live in that freedom. However, since the time Constantine, legalized religion, the church has become a place where leaders wield their power over its adherents. As a result of that, it inflicts harm on many in the name of Christ.

Although the church no longer engages in Crusades to conquer Jerusalem nor burns those it calls heretics on the stake, it still participates in modern-day witch hunts and, on a regular basis, it labels those who disagree with the doctrines of men as heretics. It wounds many whom it enslaves. When some people's eyes are opened to Christ's truth, they are driven from many churches by leaders wielding their version of scripture.

When I hear a preacher saying, "I only preach the Bible," my cautionary flag immediately goes up. I know from experience that means he or she only teaches the parts of the Bible with which they agree, those which support their doctrine. The rest will be ignored or twisted to fit their point of view.

The one thing missing from most churches is the leadership of the Holy Spirit. Even some Pentecostals (people who emphasize a relationship with the Holy Spirit) place themselves under the law. Many look for rules to obey instead of following the Spirit.

The church in which I, at the age of ten, was baptized never mentioned the Holy Spirit, and the one where I spent many of my adult years gave only lip service to him. Their doctrine allowed them to talk about him, but not to believe in him. The Holy Spirit is the only one who can heal our wounds and the only one who can prevent them from happening.

Equipping the Body

When I hear pastors talk about the deficiencies of their people, I wonder, *whose fault is that?* As the spiritual head of the church, it is the pastor's responsibility to see that they are not deficient. God gave to the church apostles, prophets, evangelists, pastors, and teachers for the equipping of the saints to do the work of the ministry, for the edifying of the body of Christ (Eph 4:11-12). If the people of a church are deficient in their understanding, in their skill, or in any other way, the fault is the pastor's. He or she is the spiritual head of the church.

How then should we pray for the pastor? First, we should not judge him or her by our prayers. I made that mistake once. One morning I was praying *about* my pastor instead of praying *for* him. I made a series of judgments and requested God to change each of those faults in him. As I finished making my accusations, the Holy Spirit caused me to begin speaking in tongues. When he finished, I was given the interpretation. As I continued my prayer, I heard myself repeating each of the accusations I had made, and adding to it the statement, "And I am just like that."

When that ended, the Holy Spirit spoke and said, "I have put you together because iron sharpens iron, and you will love him. This is your warning."

I was tempted to say, "You might as well kill me now. I can't do that." Fortunately, my brain overcame my emotion, and I heard myself say, "You will have to help me with that. I can't do it on my own."

From that experience, I learned two things: I learned to pray for someone, not about them; and I learned just how completely God's love can cover our faults. Because of God's supernatural love given to me at that very moment, I loved that man until his death. Even though we had many contentious encounters, from that time on I was never critical of him, only concerned for him.

When we pray for our pastors, it should always be for them, not about them. We should ask God to bless them and to protect them from the wiles of the devil. When he does that for them, they will bless us. If your pastor is stubborn and doesn't listen to the people, pray that God will make the pastor as pliable putty in his hands. Ask that the pastor's ears be opened to the slightest whisper of the Holy Spirit. In that way, he or she will hear God and bless the church.

If your pastor feels the need to be in control of every little thing, it probably stems from a feeling of insecurity or a spirit of distrust. Pray that he or she will learn to trust in God, and come to realize that God can provide for the church the help they need for the jobs that need to be done. Ask God to allow the pastor to feel his love and ask that he give the pastor the heart and mind of Christ.

If your pastor is deficient in anything, pray and give thanks to God for providing that which they need to do the work. There is a pretty good chance that those who pray for the pastor will not spend their time being critical of the pastor. The things that we pray for our pastors should also be those which we pray for the teachers and the elders of our church. When these people are blessed by God to do their jobs, we are blessed by the job they do.

Paul said that we wrestle not against flesh and blood, but against powers and principalities, the rulers of the darkness of this age and spiritual hosts of wickedness in heavenly places (Eph 6:12). He also said that the goal of ministry was to make known to those powers and principalities the manifold wisdom of God (Eph 3:10). When conflict occurs in the church, it is imperative to remember that the war is not with each other but with the demonic powers that will take advantage of our weaknesses and exploit them to their advantage.

Forces Against the Church

The church is beset by three forces. The first force is the natural proclivity of mankind to desire its own way. Pastors want things their way, and many try to get their way by cajoling, manipulating, and coercing the membership of their church. When that happens, the elders of the church should recognize it and put a stop to it as soon as possible. It should be done in love.

Sometimes strong-willed elders or other members of the church want to have their way; in those cases, it is the responsibility of the pastor to address the problem, in a loving way, quickly. If the leadership teams of the church understood that it is God's church and that it is his will that must be done, Satan and his demons would be on notice regarding the wisdom of God's plan (Eph 3:10).

The second force is lust. Sometimes pastors and other leaders give in to their own desires of the flesh and harm the faith of many. If or when repentance occurs, the members need to forgive and to enable restoration through that forgiveness. We should always look at what is in our own heart before we cast a stone because of what is in someone else's heart. Pastors or church members who repent and seek forgiveness for their transgressions should be restored instead of shunned.

The third force is demonic oppression. The most destructive enemies of the church are powers in heavenly places. These demonic forces will destroy a church, and they must be dealt with by the power of the Holy Spirit. One of these is the spirit of Absalom. Absalom was a son of David. Because his half-brother had forced himself upon Tamar, Absalom's sister, Absalom plotted revenge upon his brother and killed him.

Later, Absalom sought the help of one of David's lieutenants and convinced him to talk David into letting him return to Jerusalem. After David brought Absalom to Jerusalem, he did not grant him an audience for two years. Jealousy took hold in Absalom's heart. He felt slighted by his father. That, combined with a penchant for revenge, caused him to undermine David with the people in his kingdom; in time, Absalom led a revolt against his father, David. This story is found in 2 Samuel, beginning in chapter 13. This spirit of Absalom works from a desire for revenge and from jealousy. It gives people the desire to possess another's authority and position. It uses members of the church to undermine the pastor.

The Jezebel Spirit

Another power—and one that is probably the most destructive and difficult to deal with—is the spirit of Jezebel. This one desires not to turn the people against the pastor but tries to turn him against the people. Jezebel was the wife of King Ahab. She exercised power over the king. She worshiped Baal and made war on all of God's prophets. This spirit usually enters the church through someone who is not a Christian but pretends to be. In the one instance that I experienced, this demon came through a practicing witch pretending to be a Christian.

When this spirit gains influence over the pastor, all the weaknesses of his heart will come to the surface. His lust for control will cause him to manipulate and twist the Word of God just enough to mislead the fellowship. He will impugn the motives of those who question him. He will drive off those who cared for the man he was before Jezebel. In some instances, sexual sin becomes a problem. Like Jim Jones, he will lead many to "drink the Kool-Aid."

Most of the time, the danger of what that pastor is doing will go unnoticed by the leaders of the church. They are under the Jezebel spell. Gradually one leader at a time will see the truth but will be unable to enlist the help of those whose eyes are blinded. By the time eyes are finally opened to the facts, many in the church will have left. The finances will be in trouble, and great harm will have been done to the faith of many.

When church leadership decides to deal with this problem, the pastor will probably take many of the remaining members and try to start another church, which of course will fail. This spirit is challenging to deal with. She is cunning and very deceptive and, at the same time, very destructive. Because the pastor is the one she possesses, spiritual leadership is not forthcoming. The Holy Spirit is limited in how he can work.

The purpose of each of these spirits is to destroy the church, either by deposing the pastor or by claiming the pastor. Unfortunately, because some leaders do not understand the spiritual realm, they choose to respond in a fleshly manner. In a short time, members will be turned against each other, and the demonic will win.

Remove the Log in Your Eye

I am convinced that the first step every church should take when dissension rears its ugly head is to have a meeting between the pastor and the church members involved. The pastor must understand his or her role in their criticisms; much of the time the member is crying out because of their need, and only when they feel ignored does the cry turn to blame. Before these meetings, the pastor and the member should put on the girdle of truth. Each should look at the log in their own eye.

The member's goal must be to bless the pastor not to condemn the pastor. The pastor's intent should be to listen with a heart of compassion while wearing the girdle of truth. If that does not solve the problem, the Bible says that a church meeting should occur (Mt 18:15-17). I believe everyone should be allowed to express his or her feelings.

Some pastors will not do this because they fear losing control of the meeting, or because they refuse to face their own role in the problems of the church. If they were to realize that God is in control and were willing to leave it to God, I believe it would work out, even if it seemed that chaos might rule. I know it would if spiritual principles had been taught to the people and were applied in the meeting.

God always has cool heads present—people who at the right moment can share a Word of wisdom. If the things being expressed were about the pastor, it is the pastor's responsibility to self-judge. If guilty, the pastor should confess all faults to the congregation and ask for forgiveness. The pastor should not make excuses for these mistakes. If not guilty, the pastor should trust God for defense.

In One Accord

When members are told they can't talk about the problems they see in the church, it makes things worse. Perception is the reality in the minds of many. To correct that reality their opinions must be changed. That begins by hearing opposing points of view.

No problem in the church can be solved by talk alone or by forbidding the expression of opinion. After people have had their say, group prayer must occur. It must be unceasing and committed prayer, by the body in one accord. Many churches have what they call a Wednesday night prayer and Bible study. In most, it is neither prayer nor Bible study. Prayer is an afterthought, and the Bible study is nothing more than a recycled sermon and a time that allows questions and answers.

If pastors understood they have nothing to say that is more important than prayer, these Wednesday night meetings might accomplish something. If these pastors who say they only preach the Bible would practice what is in the Bible, their churches would indeed put the powers of evil in heavenly places on notice. In the early church, prayer opened the doors of prisons, and angels set Peter and others free from those prisons (Acts 12:5-10, 16:26).

Many times the names of the sick are mentioned in these Wednesday meetings, and the people present are asked to go home and pray for them. They should. But the Bible says that the sick should present themselves to the elders and be anointed with oil and prayed for (Jas 5:14). In this way, many are healed. When has your church done that?

When the church engages in collective prayer, the power of the Holy Spirit is magnified. The larger the number of Christians praying in one accord, the greater is the presence and power of the Holy Spirit. When God's people who are called by his name *humble* themselves and *pray* and *seek* his face and *turn* from their wicked ways, then he *promises* to hear from heaven and to *forgive* their sin and to *heal* their land (2 Chr 7:14). Churches whose members come together and pray in one accord send the demons running.

I know this works. In one church where I was chairman of the deacons, we had a severe budget shortage. We came together in prayer, in one accord, and confessed the shortcomings of our fellowship and sought the Lord's face. The very next week our giving went up dramatically, and the budget was soon balanced.

What I am attempting to get across is that the demonic and the flesh would not have their way in our churches if the pastors did their job. If they taught their people to pray and if it was practiced in a corporate setting, the Holy Spirit would prevail, and the demons would flee.

Pray for Your Pastors

Some readers may think my comments are unusually harsh regarding pastors. I do not want it to seem that way. I have known many and worked with many in my lifetime. My father-in-law was one. The pastor has a difficult and challenging job. They are judged by the membership every Sunday and held accountable by them. God holds them responsible as shepherds. Fortunately, he is more merciful than many church members. Pastors try to please the membership and God. Because their livelihood is dependent upon the church, they walk a tightrope between God and the people.

The best prayers we can offer for them are prayers for protection from Satan. We need to continually pray that they will hear the soft whisper of the Holy Spirit and listen to his voice. Ask that the eyes of their understanding will be open to the truth. Pray that people who are crying out will be heard and that their cries will be understood as cries of need, not as cries of criticism. Pray that their people will have Christ's unfailing love for them. Pray that they will have that same love for the people. Love will cover all of our faults. Remember the laws of God's kingdom. Blessed are the merciful for they will obtain mercy (Mt 5:7).

There is no more difficult job than that of a pastor (except child rearing). The way they do their job blesses many and can harm even more. We must learn to pray for them daily. We should never judge them but should always bless them through our prayers. The Lord takes pleasure in those who fear him and in those who hope for mercy (Ps 147:11). Fear of God is having proper respect for who he is. In that light, pray for mercy upon the pastor and pray for the pastors, not about them; in doing that, God will show you mercy.

Healing Wounds by the Church

The most rabid, anti-religion, anti-Christian, anti-God people I have met are the ones who were wounded by the church. Their children are the most resistant people to the plan of salvation that I have encountered. It is challenging to restore faith into someone whose belief system has been shattered. Three things must happen before that can occur.

First, time must elapse. It takes time for the emotions to settle and for the pain to subside. That could be years for some. When the true believers' faith is shaken, that pain goes deep, and it causes them to put up many thick, tall, and impenetrable walls around their heart.

The second thing that must happen is for stink-n think-n to change. Because true believers think that God is in charge of the church, it is easy for Satan to cause them to believe that the faults of the Church are God's will: that he either endorsed the behavior, that he doesn't care, or that he doesn't have the power to prevent the problems.

God may be in charge of the overall Church, but in some instances, he has no control over the local church. The god of some pulpits is the god of this world. The shepherd of some churches is no more than a wolf in sheep's clothing. Sometimes, the shepherd's character and faith are being tested by Satan just as our own is tested. In all cases, God has given us free will and freedom of choice. He will not interfere. But with prayer, Jesus will intercede.

When that stink-n think-n is changed, the third thing can happen. Restoration can occur; but only as a result of forgiveness. Christ died on a Cross so that we could be forgiven for our sins and restored to a relationship with the triune Godhead. The only way any spiritual healing can occur is first for forgiveness to happen. Then restoration is possible. Remember the laws of the kingdom are applicable. Who must we forgive? We must forgive the source of our pain.

Some of us need to forgive God. In some situations, that is the only way our stink-n think-n can be changed. As long as we think God is at fault, we will never understand who the real enemy is. It takes audacity to forgive God. I recommend humility in the process.

Be honest, but not accusatory. Say, "Father, I am hurt, and I am angry. I need your help to understand what happened. I want to let go of my hurt, my anger, and my doubt. I forgive you for the pain I feel and ask that you show me your truth. I don't just want to restore the relationship we had; but because you are refining my faith through this experience, I want a faith that is better. Please forgive me, Father, because I forgive you."

God has big shoulders, he feels our pain, and he responds to cries for help. Just remember, when you cry out, to whom you are speaking.

When I was in this situation, God couldn't restore my relationship with him until I prayed that prayer. Even though I knew in my mind that he wasn't at fault for the pain I felt, in my heart I blamed him. It was his church that caused the problem. Why did he allow it to happen? I told him what was happening. I pleaded for his help. Why didn't he do something? Those were the foolish cries of a young man lacking in experience and understanding. All restoration begins with forgiveness. Understanding comes later.

Forgiveness and Restoration

If you are one of those wounded by a church or by an act of unspeakable cruelty perpetrated upon you in a physical way, please don't allow your pain to place a curse upon your bloodline for all eternity. Deal with your pain now. Allow the Holy Spirit to work with you. Ask God to bind Satan and his lies and release the Holy Spirit to redeem and restore your relationship with him. It may take some time, and he may need to place you back into a church or even into the one that caused the problem to complete the process. You may need to confront whoever harmed you and forgive them face to face. Trust God to make the right choices and allow him to put his arms around you. He is the best doctor I know.

Chapter 15
Praying to Win

When I told a friend that I was writing a book entitled *Praying to Win*, his question was, "Praying to win what?" My answer is "Praying to win the war." It is time for Christians to decide what they want. Patrick Henry said,

> Is life so dear, or peace so sweet, as to be purchased at
> the price of chains and slavery? Forbid it. Almighty God,
> I know not what course others may take. But as for me,
> give me liberty or give me death.

It is time for Christians to decide which they prefer: the chains of slavery to sin or the liberty of life in Christ. It is time to determine if they prefer the bondage of religion or the freedom of life in the Holy Spirit. It is time to decide if they want to put on the new man, which after God is created in righteousness and true holiness (Eph 4:24). I challenge those who read this book to make that choice.

Most of my life, I have lost the battles that I should have won. Thankfully, I have not lost the war. The Patriots in the Revolutionary War lost most of the actions they fought—until Yorktown. They won that battle, and with it the war. On the Cross, Jesus won the war of redemption; but on our knees, we must win the battles.

The first step in winning those battles is to exchange our stink-n think-n for the correct understanding. Those who have accepted the sacrifice Jesus made on the Cross and who have received the Holy Spirit are no longer sinners in the eyes of God. The blood Jesus shed for us washes us clean and covers all our sins (Heb 9:14, 22, 10:19, 13:12; Rv 1:5). Not just some of them. If you are listening to a preacher who continually says that you are an unworthy sinner—quit listening. That one does not understand grace and has not learned to live in the freedom of the Holy Spirit.

Jesus did not die so that we could remain sinners. When he comes into our heart, we are transformed into saints who occasionally sin. It is time for us to understand that Jesus did not die so that we could be sinners who are saved but saints who are worth keeping. Instead of confessing every little sin you have committed, each time you pray ask to be forgiven for all the sins you are guilty of (God already knows what they are), and instead, focus your prayer on the change of heart you need to keep from committing those sins.

Jesus taught that every sin comes from the heart. Peter said to repent of your wickedness, and pray to God that the thoughts of your heart may be forgiven (Acts 8:22). Don't worry about the sin; focus instead on the condition of the heart that led to it. Paul taught that we should be renewed in the spirit of our mind (Eph 4:23). It is time to quit thinking as sinners under bondage to the law and religion and to believe as saints set free from sin and to allow the Holy Spirit to incorporate the law into your heart, so you can indeed be free.

When I was a young man, the church used to sing a song about going to war. It went something like this: *Onward, Christian soldiers, marching as to war.* It is time Christians quit running from the war and begin instead to run toward the battle. Instead of running from the fight, we need to put on the whole armor of God and engage the enemy as victors. It is impossible to win the battle without first putting on the armor and without fighting in the heavenly realm.

Learn to pray with the authority Christ gave to you. Understand that whatever we ask for, in the "name of Jesus," he has promised the Father will give to us (Jn 15:16) Learn the rules of the kingdom and incorporate them into your prayer life so that the Father can answer your prayers. Remember that God is constrained by the laws of the kingdom just as we are.

The first law of the kingdom is that we love God with all our heart, mind, and soul and that we love our neighbor as ourselves. The one problem with the second part of that commandment is that some Christians don't love or like themselves. When you quit believing that you are an unworthy sinner and understand that Christ loved you enough to die for you, the Holy Spirit can turn that stink-n think-n around. When you are renewed in the spirit of your mind, you will love both yourself and your neighbor. Pray that you can have the heart and mind of Christ, and allow the Holy Spirit to make the changes he chooses.

Don't let Satan have charge over your family. Pray every day that God will put a hedge of thorns around your family as he did with Job's. Satan loves to tear apart families, and we allow him to get away with it. Instead of being angry at your spouse and harboring ill thoughts, ask God to enable you to love your spouse with his supernatural love. He will. His love covers a multitude of sins.

Instead of telling your children who they can associate with, try the wedge prayer. At times our children had friends of whom my wife and I did not approve. When that was the case, we prayed the "wedge" prayer. We asked the Lord to drive a wedge between our child and their friend if he agreed with us. Unless he had a purpose for the relationship, we asked him to place between them a wedge. Once that was prayed, my daughter never kept a boyfriend for more than two weeks. I was always amazed at how quickly and effectively God answered that prayer. Satan did not have an opportunity to use our concerns to start a fight between our children and us.

When my wife and I travel, we always ask for an angel to protect our home and for one to go with us, to keep us safe as we travel. In the thirty-nine years we lived in Oregon, we never locked the doors to our home when we went someplace. Upon our return, everything was as we left it. I continually thank God for the guardian angel who watches over us (Mt 18:10).

God's Army

We have a mighty army at our service and should recognize this truth each time we pray. Our prayers open the windows of heaven, and angels take our message to God and deliver his answers to us. That is seen in the story of Jacob (Gn 28:12). In a prophetic dream, Jacob saw a ladder reaching to the heavens and angels ascending and descending from the sky to the earth and back again. Paul taught that we are at war with the spirits in the heavens; we need to enlist our angels to carry out the fight for us. Ask, and you shall receive. Learn to enlist the help of God's angels in the battle. They are God's messengers and our protectors (Lk 1:19; Mt 2:13; Ex 23:20-22). They are ministering spirits who offer encouragement and guidance (Heb 1:14; Gn 16:7). They meet out punishment, patrol the earth, and fight the forces of evil (2 Sam 24:15-17; Zech 1:9-14; Rv 20:1, 2).

Jacob's Ladder

When conflict occurs in your life, remember to pray before any confrontation occurs. Jacob was not a nice man. He stole his brother's birthright and his father's blessing. Because of that, Esau swore to kill him. Jacob was forced to leave his home and live in his mother's land for many years. While he was running from his brother, he had the dream about the ladder and enlisted God's help to make peace with Esau. As Jacob did, we must enlist God's help every time there is conflict in our lives. Before doing anything else, go to God. Then when he opens the door, go to your brother and make peace.

Rebuke and Bind Satan

Never take Satan and his demons for granted, and never misuse your authority. We have the power to overcome Satan and his dominions. Jesus was given all authority, and he passed that same authority to his disciples and in turn to us (Mt 28:18, Jn 14:12-14). In the name of Jesus, we can bind Satan and tell him to get behind us, but do not become arrogant in that.

I remember watching a famous evangelist jump around on stage in one meeting and say, "Satan is scared of this little ol' preacher. I will stomp his head." Apparently, he forgot the part about he will bruise your heel (Gn 3:15). In a month's time, that evangelist was arrested in California for soliciting sex from a prostitute.

When confronting Satan, do as Michael the archangel did. When he contended with the devil for the body of Moses, he dared not bring against him a strong accusation, but instead said, "The Lord rebuke you."(Jude 1:9). I don't address Satan directly. He hits back. I ask the Lord to bind him and to deal with him on my behalf.

Our War Chest

We have all the resources needed to win this war. We have the Holy Spirit. He is available to all who are willing to receive him. He comes with power, and he lights a fire in us that does not go out; as long as we fan the flame, he ignites. We do that by serving God and by getting on our knees before the Lord. If we spend years without seeing or talking to our spouse, our love for them will diminish. That is true with our Lord as well. The amount of love we have for our Lord is proportional to the amount of time we spend with him. How much time are you willing to invest?

What kind of warrior do you want to be? Are you the kind who puts on the whole armor of God and with feet shod in the gospel of peace goes out to conquer with love? Or are you a religionist who in self-righteousness goes out to trample the hearts of many by abusing the Word of God? Do you embrace others with the love of God or because you want brownie points in heaven? In God's kingdom, only the things that are done as a result of love count for reward; everything else is nothing more than a tinkling cymbal (1 Cor 13).

Take Your Stand

Are you willing to be available to all the power of the Holy Spirit? If so, step forward and let him be your guide, accept his challenge, and learn from him. Don't allow the fire he lights in you to dim. Learn to pray and discover what God wants from you. In doing that you will be the warrior he wants and the one you were meant to be. Christ's death on the Cross will not be wasted on someone who buries their gifts and refuses to risk using them. Christ died so that losers could be turned into winners. Instead of thinking that you are a worthless sinner, understand that his death made you a winner. Through Jesus' name, begin to take back all that is yours in the kingdom of God. Live the life of victory that is yours!

Conclusion

What a mighty God we serve!
He can and will do all things in his time.
Through Jesus, I can do all things,
because I do love him
and am called according to his purpose.

These are the words of songs and quotes from the Bible which are truths we should all understand. When I come before my mighty God and confess to him, that is what I believe, I don't want to hear him say, "Really? Is that really what you think?"

Paul said that we should pray in the Spirit and with understanding. I said that we can motivate God with our prayers but cannot manipulate him. Now I say: Don't try either! Those who come before God in humility and sincerity will have their prayers heard. In the name of Jesus, their prayers will be heard in heaven, and because of his name, they will be answered on earth as they are in heaven.

When the answer is given in heaven and delivered to earth, it can be done. Our prayers open the windows of heaven, and angels provide that answer to us (Gn 28:12). They fight our battles with demonic forces in heavenly places and hold them at bay while we accomplish God's purpose and plan on earth (Dn 10:20, 21).

If we don't ask, we can't win. If we don't seek God's will, we won't know what it is. Christ was given authority over all flesh (Jn 17:2); and in turn, he delegated authority to his disciples so they could be one with him and the Father just as Jesus and the Father were one with each other (Jn 17:22). Also, he has granted that same glory to all those who followed them (Jn 17:20). That means you and me.

It is time that Christians quit listening to those who teach how unworthy they are. Instead of allowing that teaching to make us prisoners of religion, we should understand that may have been who we were, but that we are no longer that person. The blood of Jesus has covered our sins and washed us white as snow.

If you have received the Holy Spirit since you believed, you are now set free from the law to live in the Spirit. Because of that, and because the Holy Spirit has sealed you as a child of the Holy God, all things are now possible through Christ who lives in you. It is time for you to come boldly before the throne of God and discover what his will is for you.

> *Look where you are going, because you are going where you are looking.*

When you understand how much God loves you—what the width, length, depth, and height of his love are for you—it will not be hard to spend time thanking him for what he has done for you. It will be easy to praise him for the love Christ expended in doing that. When you focus on how much you want to be like Christ, you will ask for God to give you the heart and mind of Jesus.

Instead of dwelling upon your mistakes and failures, you will confess your sins by asking him to change the things in your heart that caused them in the first place. Remember this: *Look where you are going, because you are going where you are looking.* He is the way, the truth, and the life.

We pray as we think. If we doubt, we will pray with doubt. It is time to decide what you believe and to decide who you are. The way you pray will reveal that to you and to God. Those who pray with understanding will know who they are. They have put on the helmet of salvation and are not filled with doubt. They are ready to say, "Get thee behind me, Satan!"

Those who wear the breastplate of righteousness intend to live in the kingdom of God. Instead of living for sin, they understand that kingdom living involves turning one's back on wrongdoing. These Christians desire to please God. They have discovered the value and method of waking every morning with hearts filled with peace and joy. They don't worry about the needs of the day. They are thankful for God's blessings, even before they receive them because they know Christ will provide. They have faith.

Those who put on the girdle of truth understand that it is not a device for constriction, like a woman's girdle, but that it is one for protection. Instead of constricting movement, it protects us so that in his truth we can do his will. When you believe the truth of his Word, understand that he is the same today as yesterday, and he is the same forever, you will not be misled by the doubts Satan plants into your mind.

When you recognize the sins in your heart and confess them to God, you will not be taking the bait the demons tempt you with. Those who understand that God is all truth, that God doesn't lie, don't fall prey to Satan's lies when he tries to cast doubt into their minds and attempts to deceive them through lies and tricks.

When we pick up the shield of faith, even when all seems lost and when we don't understand, we can still be grateful for all that God is doing in our life. We believe that in all things, no matter how bad they seem at that moment, God will work for good in our life, because we love him and are called according to his purpose (Rom 8:28). Satan's lies can't convince us otherwise.

His fiery darts will cause no harm (Eph 6:16). Christians who trust God will face the tests of flesh and the trials of faith with his protection. We will have his victory, and when those tests and trials end, we will be purified as gold is by fire. We will be more like Christ. The crown of life will be awarded to us.

When you pick up the sword of the Spirit—which is the Word of God—you will, with that Word, dispatch Satan and his demons by that Word. With that Word and wearing the shield of faith, you will say to the mountains of doubt, "Be moved" and they will move.

Instead of being a nonproductive fig tree, you will bear much fruit, because you are the branch growing from his vine (Jn 15:5). With that combination, you will abide in him and him in you and then you will bear much fruit. That is his promise.

When your feet are shod in the gospel of peace, you will walk in love. Instead of walking in self-righteousness as religion teaches, you will walk as Christ did. How beautiful are the feet of those who preach the gospel of peace (Rom 10:15).

While wielding the sword of the spirit, you will turn the other cheek; give your shirt, as well as your cloak, to those in need.

Instead of wanting to draw blood with the sword you carry, you will give others new life by using the Word to bring them forgiveness and understanding. You will show to them the compassion that Christ gave to you. Because you understand that you can't give what you don't have, you will ask to be filled with all the fullness of Christ, which is God's love. Then you will wield that sword with love instead of condemnation.

Soul Winners

What a mighty God we serve. Through prayer, you will experience that. What love he has for you. In prayer, you will feel that. How high are his hopes for you? Through prayer, you will discover that. Prayer opens the doors of heaven so that you can achieve what he hopes for you.

Do you want to be a soul winner? Pray for others by name, daily. Be like the obnoxious widow who came before the judge demanding justice (Lk 18:3). She was unrelenting in her quest. Those who cry out to God day and night for the salvation of others will have their prayers answered. It will be credited to them who plant as it will be to those who harvest (Jn 4:37). He will send some to plow his ground, to reap his harvest, and others to make weapons of war (1 Sm 8:12).

You make those weapons of war with the prayers you bring for others. You equip those who will wield the sword of the Spirit with those weapons; and when those you pray for are harvested, you are credited with that harvest, just as is the one who wields the sword.

What a world prayer opens unto us; what miracles it works; what understanding it gives; what love we discover; what hope is fulfilled; what fellowship it brings! Why then don't we do more of it? It is not difficult. All we must do is open our hearts to the one who died for us.

Your Ally In the Battle

Jesus is the one who loves us enough to listen, never criticizes, and always understands. He was tempted in every way as we are. It takes time to make a best friend. How much time are you willing to invest in making Jesus your best friend? He gave his life for that reason; how much time will you give?

Recommended Reading

Henderson, Robert. *Operating in the Courts of Heaven: Granting God the Legal Rights to Fulfill His Passion and ... Answer Our Prayers.* Place of Publication Not Identified: Robert Henderson Ministries, 2016.

Munroe, Myles. *Rediscovering the Kingdom: Ancient Hope for Our 21st Century World.* Shippensburg, PA: Destiny Image Publishers, 2010.

Tomlin, Chris, and Darren Whitehead. *Holy Roar: 7 Words That Will Change the Way Your Worship.* Nashville, Tennessee.: Bowyer & Bow, 2017.

www.ingramcontent.com/pod-product-compliance
Lightning Source LLC
Chambersburg PA
CBHW060833050426
42453CB00008B/680